The Art of Being a Creature

The Art of Being a Creature

Meditations on Humus and Humility

RAGAN SUTTERFIELD

CASCADE *Books* • Eugene, Oregon

THE ART OF BEING A CREATURE
Meditations on Humus and Humility

Copyright © 2024 Ragan Sutterfield. All rights reserved. Except for brief quotations in critical publications or reviews, no part of this book may be reproduced in any manner without prior written permission from the publisher. Write: Permissions, Wipf and Stock Publishers, 199 W. 8th Ave., Suite 3, Eugene, OR 97401.

Cascade Books
An Imprint of Wipf and Stock Publishers
199 W. 8th Ave., Suite 3
Eugene, OR 97401

www.wipfandstock.com

PAPERBACK ISBN: 978-1-6667-3076-0
HARDCOVER ISBN: 978-1-6667-2266-6
EBOOK ISBN: 978-1-6667-2267-3

Cataloguing-in-Publication data:

Names: Sutterfield, Ragan, author.

Title: The art of being a creature : meditations on humus and humility / Ragan Sutterfield.

Description: Eugene, OR : Cascade Books, 2024 | Includes bibliographical references.

Identifiers: ISBN 978-1-6667-3076-0 (paperback) | ISBN 978-1-6667-2266-6 (hardcover) | ISBN 978-1-6667-2267-3 (ebook)

Subjects: LCSH: Human ecology— Religious aspects—Christianity. | Creation. | Theological anthropology—Christianity.

Classification: BT695.5 .S88 2024 (paperback) | BT695.5 .S88 (ebook)

Excerpts from T. S. Eliot's "East Coker" are from *Collected Poems,* 1909–1962 by T. S. Eliot. Copyright © 1963 by T. S. Eliot. Used by permission of HarperCollins Publishers.

05/08/24

To Emily, Lillian, and Lucia for making a home with me on this soil.

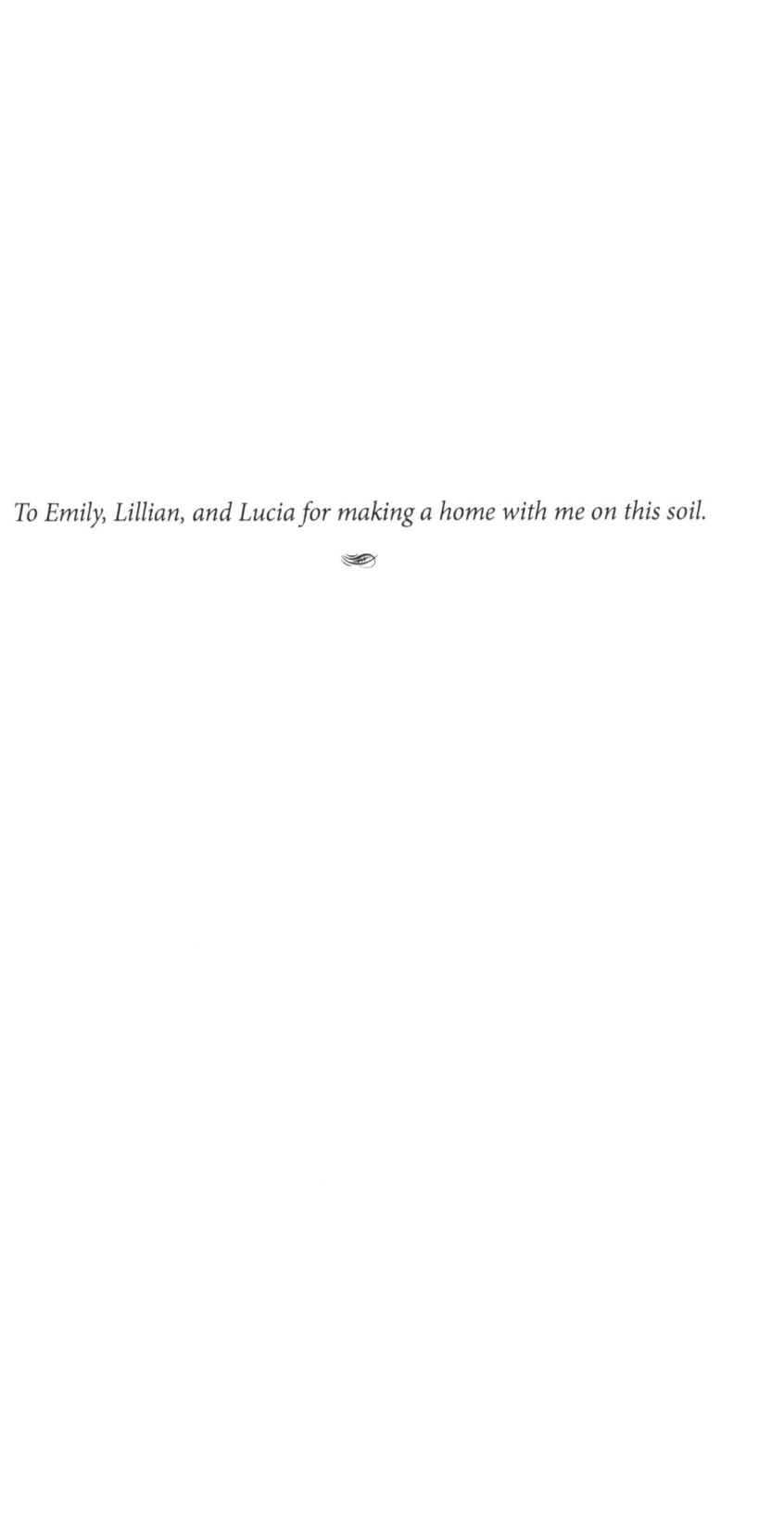

Contents

Acknowledgments   ix

ANCESTORS

Clay	3
Hori Hori	5
Inheritance	9
Adam	12
Dirt	16
Till and Keep?	19
Scything and Reaping	24
The Restless City	28
The Place of Love	31
Powers and Repentance	36

HUMILITY

Anaerobic	45
Compost and Contemplation	49
The Death of a Ewe	52
The Shadow of Death	55
Look to You	59
The Hospitality of Bread	62
Ash Wednesday	65
Last Wishes	70
Dung Beetles	72

CONTENTS

A Drain Straight to the Earth ... 74
Borders of the Holy ... 78
Scum of the Earth ... 81
The Grail of the World ... 85

RETURN

Sent Your Son ... 91
Blue Christmas ... 97
Kenotic Ecology ... 101
Thoughts While Pushing a Wheelbarrow ... 104
Fear and Grace ... 109
Awe, Awe, Awe ... 113
We Have What We Need ... 116
Skill ... 121
The Bread of Heaven ... 126
Affluence and Abundance ... 130
Sympathy ... 137
Reading the Ground ... 139
The Valley of Solidarity ... 142
Even on the Hilltops ... 145
Pruning to Pattern ... 147
The Obedience of Trees ... 150
Theosis ... 155
Paradise Lot ... 158
Forever Work ... 162

Bibliography ... 167

Acknowledgments

This book began as a Pastoral Study Project funded by the Louisville Institute. I am thankful to the institute and its staff, particularly the director at the time, Don Richter. The funding from that project allowed me to engage the writing mentorship of Paul Kingsnorth. Over the course of our work together, the conversation went well beyond the scope of this project, for which I am grateful. I've benefited from several conversation partners, many of whom provided feedback on portions of this book. Thank you to C. Christopher Smith, Jonathan Bailey, Debra Dean Murphy, and Keith Harvey for your careful reading of early drafts. James Matthews is owed particular gratitude for his careful proofing of the final manuscript. Thanks also to Kate Alexander, the Rector of Christ Episcopal Church, where I serve as a priest. Kate encouraged my work on this project and was always ready to give me the time and space to continue the work. This book would not be what it is without Christ Church, especially our "wild church" community that worships in the woods of Allsopp Park, bringing our faith close to the ground. My daughters, Lillian and Lucia, who will inherit for both good and ill what I've received and passed on to them, have been my partners in turning compost, planting gardens, and exploring the wonders of the given world. I hope that this book will be a help to them as they learn to live human lives in an inhuman age. Finally, I could not have written this without Emily Sutterfield. Our morning conversations, Emily's clear-eyed edits, and the work of making a home together over these past years all made this book what it is in all its best parts. It is to her and our daughters that this book is dedicated.

Ancestors

Home is the place of my attention.
TERRY TEMPEST WILLIAMS, *EROSION: ESSAYS OF UNDOING*

Nothing left on the continent even hints at what has gone. All replaced now, by thousands of miles of continuous backyards and farms with thin lines of second growth between them. Still, the soil remembers, for a little while longer, the vanished woods and the progress that unmade them. And the soil's memory feeds their backyard pine.
RICHARD POWERS, *THE OVERSTORY: A NOVEL*

. . . truthful self-knowledge is at the heart of the virtue of humility.
STANLEY HAUERWAS, *THE CHARACTER OF VIRTUE*

Clay

Here it is red, white, and gray, veins running close to the surface. Dig half a foot and clay begins to show, a slimy mix easily rubbed into a ball. Where the creeks have run for any length of time, the banks are made of its mud, rocks jutting out here and there, the ancient sediments becoming slick in the rain. Mixed in are layers of shale, the now fossil clay of eons past when the mountains here had not yet crested. It was a shallow sea, I'm told. A few miles away I once found shark teeth in a roadside wash. Another time it was the stem of crinoid—reminders that this place has been many things before I or any of my kind came to know it.

In a soil test of the simplest kind—a bit of backyard dirt shaken in a jar of water—it is clay that is the last to fall from the suspension. Compared to sand and silt and the organic matter of dead plants and animals, it is the smallest particle of soil—a crystalline structure made from rock eroded and eroded again until it is so small it is almost elemental. That, or churned up from deep in the earth, synthesized in the heart of the planet. Both kinds exist, buttered through the layers of the ground.

Small, volatile, reactive—clay is both plastic when wet and hard when fired. Shape it into any form; then heat it until it becomes like stone. Clay tablets are the oldest known medium for writing—angled, wedge-shaped forms pressed into a flattened lump. Clay pots have been dated to 16,000 years ago. Few artifacts, save those made of stone, last so long.

I have a shard of pottery I was given as a boy, a piece a friend found broken in a field. It had been made by an indigenous person centuries or millennia before. In the pink earthenware I can see the fingerprints of the potter where she pressed her thumbs, forming a pattern like a woven basket in the plastic earth. I like to pick it up from time to time and run my fingers over her prints—a momentary connection to a past still present in clay.

Complex and abundant, malleable and ionic, clay could have been the beginning of that potter, the tree under which she sat, the dog running through the village along the riverbank. Clay could have been the beginning of us all. All those molecules of clay floating around in the earth are electric, popping with charges seeking balance. Churning in the earth, bonding together, trading electrons, perhaps, somewhere 4 billion years ago, patterns began to emerge.

There's a theory, minority but serious, that claims that clay was the beginning of life.[1] In it clay crystals began to shape their environments in small ways—*sign of life one*. Then, those patterns began to be replicated using "low-tech genes"—*sign of life two*. With time, the reactions became more complex, amino acids and nucleic acids were synthesized and incorporated. It was like kindling—dry, brittle, ready for a blaze. Then the fire. The spark of the Spirit brooding over the waters, a random catalyst in the ground—somehow, someway, life began from dead matter, the elements synthesized in the nuclear fission of stars gathered into something altogether new.

From there we imagine a life that continued to push toward the surface, some amphibious creature crawling out from the primordial soup. We are oriented to the surface, and that's where we center the story, the great leap of life, but our true source remains in the depths. The life we see and interact with day to day—the trees and people and pets, the birds in our yards, the rabbits in our gardens—those are only a small fraction of the respirating, replicating, gene-passing creatures on earth. Measured by mass, the total life beneath the surface may exceed that on top. And those of us who live on the surface, building new towers to the sky, dreaming of colonies on the moon, lives in simulation—we still depend upon the depths and live by their mercy. Somewhere there must be a body and with it a world grounded in the earth, made possible by microbes.

The ancients had it right—the human from the humus, the *adam* from the *adamah*. We do not live on earth but from it. The soil's health is ours. And for those who sense some wrong, some disease in human life with which we've all become infected, perhaps it is back to the soil that we should return to begin our healing. Maybe our hope is not in the new, in the discoveries of the latest science put to work by the most innovative technologies. Perhaps we are called to begin where we are, letting go of the temptation of long journeys and grand plans, as we learn again what is right beneath our feet. And through attention to the earth itself, we may discover the lost art of being human—creatures born from clay, spirit-filled soil.

---

1. For a discussion of this theory, see Wolfe, *Tales from the Underground*, 26–29.

Hori Hori

One April, for my birthday, I received a small tool called a hori hori. I'd seen one the previous fall, carried at the hip of an herbalist during a permaculture workshop. My wife, attuned to my hints, bought me one. It now sits on a shelf by my door, always ready to go to the garden.

Created in Japan, the tool looks like a hand spade at first. Hori hori, an onomatopoeia in Japanese for the sound the tool makes as it's pressed repeatedly into the ground, translates to "dig dig." But it is more than a shovel. On one side there is a sharpened straight blade, on the other a serrated one, and so the spade is also a knife. Its original purpose in Japan was for foraging "mountain vegetables," wild plants growing with only the work of rain and wind and soil. Foragers could cut mushrooms and stalks or dig in the soil to pull up tubers and truffles. Gardeners have found it is good for weeding, planting, trimming here and there—a tool for the daily work of walking about, seeing what needs doing.

I mostly use my hori hori with knees bent, shoulders stooped toward the ground. Unlike the long-handled tools of shovel, hoe and rake, broad and garden forks, the hori hori encourages close encounters. It is a tool for careful attention. With every tool there is a framing, an orientation. The hammer searches for a nail, the car a road, the book a mind. The hori hori pushes into the ground, a key in the surface, opening the depths.

We have a strip of perennial herbs and flowers bordering the street—a hedge of flavor, healing, and beauty. I mulch it, lay newspaper and cardboard around the plants, but still Bermuda grass finds a way. I use my hori hori to work down beneath a tendril, tearing a long stretch of grass from the mulched bed.

With each uprooting I see the varied life within the soil, gathered around the white roots and rhizomes. Earthworms and grubs, spiders hunting at the borders, pill bugs rolled into their defensive balls—this soil is home to the small and unseen lives those of us who tower above rarely attend to. Beneath the wood chips I often find white filament, spreading like subterranean spider webs. These are the branches of mycorrhizal fungi, working to turn the mulch to new earth, connecting the plants to one another, trading the minerals broken free from the ground for the sugars plants have made from sunlight. Everything here is eating and dying, growing and birthing—life upon life.

It feels good to work here with my hori hori, bent over the soil. There is some sense that this is what I was made for, cultivating the ground, tending life. It feels both human and godlike, and perhaps that is what it is, for we are a mix of earth and image, a reflection of God made from the ground.

I grew up with the stories—creation in six days, rest on the seventh. Then Adam and Eve in the garden, living among the animals in a peaceable kingdom until all was lost through the fatal bite. Cartoons of creation in a children's Bible. There was a kind of magic to it then, a sense of myth and deep time until the adults started trying to make it into a defensible point of scientific fact. It was only after much study that I found the magic again, unfolding the layers to hear the stories in their brilliant imagination—the truth of who we are.

I began to hear, in some ancient echo, the hymn of a priest around the fire, singing on the banks of a river in Babylon. Gathered around were people, captive and exiled, trying to understand who they were. Many of them had known no land but Babylon, no faith but what they could work out in the borders on these Saturday evenings, weeping by the water. They asked the questions we all ask—who are we, what is the world, how did it all come to be? And like the wisest elders, this priest offered a story.

In that story, sung from memory like the stanzas of the blind poet Homer, was the creation of the cosmos. The priest, or some poet of his class, had been working it out—a counter song of creation, sung against the stories of their captors. What is the world? A temple. Who are we? Priests. To a priest with no temple and a people with no land, such a hymn offered a radical hope, a rearrangement of reality.

The song was offered against the stories of a world made in violence, the music of the Empire. Babylon sang of the cosmos created from the goddess Tiamat, her body cut in two, half becoming sky, the other earth. Humankind was formed from the remains of her second husband. In another of their songs the first human was the offspring of an incestuous god who impregnated his granddaughter. *The Epic of Gilgamesh*, oldest of the myths of Babylon, told of a wild creature, apelike and hairy, made human through a visit to a prostitute. In all of these ancient stories, creation was accidental, chaotic, a divine afterthought at best. These were stories that fit a world of violence and caprice; of constantly changing favors.

Beresit bara Elohim et hasamayim weet ha'ares, sang the poet by the river. *In the beginning God created the heavens and the earth.* This new song offered a different pattern, playing with the Hebrew poetry of math, sevens upon sevens—it signals to the attentive listener a word of its purpose. Creation is not chaotic. Creation is formed as a temple, a cosmic dwelling for God. Like the tabernacle in the wilderness made in seven days; the temple Solomon built in seven years, the whole world of creation was made in six days with the seventh, the sanctification of time, completing it. The whole of our existence as we live and know it, played out in the four dimensions of our experience of reality, is a place of God's dwelling, a place that invites worship. God was there, even in Babylon; God is here even in a garden bed beside the street of a southern city.

Who are we? The song continued. *Then God said, "Let us make humanity in our image to resemble us so that they may take charge of the fish of the sea, the birds in the sky, the livestock, all the earth, and all the crawling things on earth."* Look around, the poet gestured—the face of the old man, weathered by the anxieties of exile; the young woman, body reclined against her lover, within her the possibility of birth; the child playing by the stream, her hands cupped ready to capture a tadpole—look at them and see something of God reflected in the world; creatures granted some of God's own power to form and shape and call the world toward wholeness. To be human is to be the connecting point of the divine and earthly, to see the world in its potential, flourishing mass, and offer it as a gift back to God.

Someone on the bank may have heard these words and remembered the stark prayer that David had offered at the end of his reign, in those days when Israel was whole, and division and exile were still far off:

> Who am I,
> and who are my people,
> that we should be able to offer so willingly?
> Since everything comes from you,

we have given you that which comes from your own hand.
To be sure, we are like all our ancestors,
 immigrants without permanent homes.
Our days are like a shadow on the ground,
 and there's no hope.[1]

To be a priest in the ancient patterns of Israel was to offer only what was already given; to return in sacred acknowledgment the things received—all both living breath and fleeting vapor. The priests were of a landless tribe, living at the mercy of their neighbors. And so, it seemed, this creation song was saying we all are in the end. The world is not of our making; we can make no claim to possess it. Our dominion is not that of possessors doing what we want, but rather a call to worship, a call of all creation to be made whole in the common song of obedience to God.

To be human is to be a priest, receiving the gift and naming the holy. To tend the soil, to bend the blade of the hori hori over the earth was to reflect in some way this ancient call. It was a sacrifice in the truest sense of that word: *sacra-facere*, sacred-making. Digging in the garden, in this small holy moment, I was acting as a priest calling creation to its wholeness, making way for its flourishing in a small space bordered by asphalt. I was recognizing the ground it already was—a holy gift. But such a gift was not easily visible everywhere. There was the sacred and desecrated, side by side.

---

1. 1 Chr 29:14–15 CEB.

Inheritance

Our home place is not large by any agricultural standards. It is a small house and typical lot in the urban core of my city, a bit more than a tenth of an acre. There is a large Catalpa tree in the backyard that flowers in the spring, shedding its petals like snow across the grass. In June the undersides of its leaves come alive with large green and black caterpillars, adapted as most caterpillars are to eat only the leaves of one species of tree. In a few weeks these caterpillars will take wing in the night as Catalpa Sphinx moths, hovering like hummingbirds over the flowers of our yard.

The bark of our Catalpa is pocked with sapsucker wells, all arranged in neat lines. Sapsuckers are a kind of woodpecker that spend their winters in Arkansas, disappearing in March and returning in October. They tap the sap like maple syrup wells, drilling holes and feeding on the sugar. As they move from tree to tree, the woodpeckers spread fungal spores, like heartwood rot—ensuring future nesting cavities and keeping the forest going in its dance of succession, death and life again.

Not far from the Catalpa, beside the back fence, there once stood a giant oak. It shaded the house and much of the backyard. Looked at from old satellite photos it covered most of the house in a merciful green. The tree had heartwood rot, hidden to all but an expert's eye. One night in a storm a few years ago the hollow core was revealed as the whole mass of the tree came crashing down across the yard and smashing the back windows of the laundry room.

Now it is a hollow stump around which reishi mushrooms grow, feeding on the stump and the rotting roots beneath the surface. I collect the mushrooms and boil their stiff fruit in water, then soak them in vodka. The result is a tincture meant to boost the immune system. I take a few drops in water through the cold season. I do not know if it works, but I like this act of collecting medicine from my yard, free for the taking.

Reishi and other fungi that cause heart rot can be found here. Most are invisible, showing themselves only when they fruit in mushroom form. All of them are at work, in the soil, in trees, in the fallen grass—decomposing the world into new forms, the basic elements necessary for life. Without them everything would simply be a fossilized skeleton of past life and the soil would have little to offer plants for new growth. But with the help of fungi, wood rots into soil, bodies break into humus, and rock is broken down into new earth.

We bought this house with the proceeds of rot and rock. Beneath what are now the pine woods near Camden, Arkansas, a cretaceous sea accumulated algae and plankton, mollusks and mosasaurs. Over generations, their bodies settled beneath the water, sediments entombing them in mud and silt, lime and sand. With time, the sediments turned to stone, the gas of the decaying life filling subterranean pockets in the earth. The bodies, their carbons gathered into oil, became black pools and lakes, filling reservoirs in the rock.

My wife's great aunt owned an acreage near Camden. On it were several wells, tapped into the ancient oil lakes beneath, rigs resembling giant iron horses galloping to pump the crude into tanks. My wife, Emily, had known and loved this aunt, often going to her house and staying, sitting with her in her quiet home watching birds out the window. This aunt had no children of her own, and so when she died, she left a share of the well leases to Emily and her siblings.

With a few signatures of documents in the mail, we were now involved, improbably, in a small share of oil wealth. Every month or so we'd get a check for a few hundred dollars deposited into our account. When the price of oil was high, the check would be larger. When it was low, smaller. Either way, it was always a useful supplement.

Though the money was helpful, we always felt conflicted about the checks. Oil—its burning, the machine power it enables—has long been in conflict with the systems of life. And though we were as entangled in its use as anyone else, we hoped for and sought another way. It is one thing to be trapped in an economy with which you fundamentally disagree; it is quite another to actively profit from it. Yet that is where we found ourselves.

We couldn't stop the well. Maybe if we'd been more radical, we'd have cashed in the shares and given the money to bail out pipeline blockaders.

INHERITANCE

Instead, we sold the lease, stopping the direct deposits of this abstract economy, and made the down payment on our home.

It was an imperfect move, but it began what I hope is a different kind of life. We all have inheritances, and we must deal with them, one way or another. It seemed fitting to turn the abstractions of the economy, the strange ownership of the ground beneath the ground, to buy a real place where we could make and maintain a living. We were trying, in some small way, to change our inheritance—to push it back from the market and toward the soil, to cultivate a place of care and creation, a home even in the midst of the city.

Adam

The other night my daughters were comparing toes. One's longest is just next to the big toe, extending out past all the rest. For the other, her big toe is the longest. It is a heritable difference, like attached and unattached ear lobes. I remember learning about these common genetic traits along with Gregor Mendel's peas while sitting in the hard plastic desks of high school.

Genetic differences are the inheritances of the body—the coded patterns we pass down. But our bodies are also made by our context, our environment, our experiences and communities. There are human communities, yes, but there are also microbes in us and around us. The bacteria in our gut alone can regulate up to 30 percent of the chemicals that circulate in our bodies. These microbes can make a difference in which genes are turned on or off, expressed or unexpressed, and many of them were inherited from our parents as our mothers nursed us and our fathers kissed us.

Then there is the nurture and trauma we experience at home or in our world; racism and poverty, violence and abuse, care and resilience, stories and art—all of these have their effects on the expression of our genes. And this is to say nothing of the larger inheritances of our culture and our economy. Each is the accumulation of thousands of decisions from the question of what we can eat or should wear, to how we might extend our power or make use of our limited resources.

Our inheritances—bodily, cultural, ecological—form our options, they are the things we carry into the world. The question becomes, what do we do with our inheritances? What are we to make of our ancestors?

After the story of the cosmos as a temple, human beings as the priests of all creation, the poet stopped his hymn. Now, from the edge, there was another voice—older, grittier, earthy. This wasn't the high poetry of the priest, instead it had the feel of a storyteller, long practiced, drawing images from the embers of the gathered fire. Here the beginning was not cosmic, but local—a garden where animal and human bodies were made from soil, God bent over the earth to breathe life into the ground. In this second story, the ancestors are not general types. They are concrete and particular—they have names. It starts with Adam, the humus-being, named for the earth from which he was made—*adamah*, the humus soil, compost, the kind of dirt in which we can grow something.

We all have a common ground of inheritance, a common source in the soil. Your body, each cell of your skin, each synapse of your brain, every wriggling sperm or quaking egg, the pigment of your retina was made of sunlight and earth, converted into proteins and sugars, made useful by plants and animal rumens and the microbes that team inside us all.

We began as life drawn from the soil, nourished in the womb by the foods of the earth, nursed on milk made from death and decay, light and growth. Our life and the life of the soil are tied together. If it is poisoned we are poisoned. DDT, PCBs, these toxins are all commonly passed on in the milk of mothers. The chemicals we use to order the earth return to create disorder in our bodies. And yet, soil also contains the possibility of our healing and the renewal of all creation. Soil's life can transform damaged land into a flourishing home place for myriad animals; the microbes in soil and the plants that move their roots within it can undo the damage of poisons, metabolizing them into inert elements, if given enough time. The earth can repair itself if we waited and stayed still, rather than continuing the barrage.

That we live from and are deeply connected to the soil was an obvious truth to the indigenous people who first told the stories that became the Bible. For them the land spoke, it was alive, even animate. Rocks could bear witness; stones could cry out. When they wanted to name human life in its beginning, the one from whom all inheritance would come, they called the first person *adam*—Hebrew for earth-creature, one drawn from the soil.

But identity was not only a matter of classification, like the species in a field guide ordered by their varied taxonomies. Ancestors mattered. Who was your father and who was your father's father, was an important fact about you in this patriarchal culture. So in the story that answered the question of who we are, the ancient storyteller combined the basic fact of our nature with the name of our first father—we are *adam* from Adam, Adam from the *adamah*.

This common ancestor from the *adamah*, means that we share some kinship with other animals. We are all creatures first of all. Along with earth and sky, trees and lakes or even wisdom and understanding—all of these are made and ordered by God. What makes us human is not our source in the soil or the breath God breathed into us, for all creatures share in the spirit of God's life. In the older, ancient story from the edge of the fire, the one we find now in Genesis chapter 2, the human calling is made more domestic. We may be priests, but like most priests in history, we are priests with gardens to tend. The *adam*, this other story says, is made to serve and preserve the garden in which he is placed, he is to be a cultivator of life.

I recently heard it said that all sin is born from a desire not to be human. We either want to be more than human like gods or we sink below our humanity. In the ancestor stories of the Bible, we find both. From early on, these stories tell us, there has been an attempt to be more than human and less than human. We attempted to be godlike by eating the forbidden fruit and building Babel; and we were less than human through the murder and violence that brought about the Flood. In each movement, we failed in our vocation to serve and preserve the soil, we did not tend to the very source of our life.

And we have inherited it all—*adam*, the Fall, the cursed soil, Cain, and the violent roots of civilization. We have inherited oil, two centuries of burning through a million years of sunlight, the metabolites of ancient algae and towering trees, fern covered bogs—all collapsed into a black ooze long locked beneath the rock. There's no need of a title, a reading of the will—the deposits from our past keep coming into our accounts and we have to discern what to do with them, how to receive our inheritance.

For the early Christians, part of the answer came in joining a new family. This required a new ancestor, someone who could provide the pattern for human life reborn. The old earthling Adam was replaced by the human Jesus. Unlike the old human form, which forgot itself by seeking to be both more and less than it was, Christ lived into the pattern that would lead to humanity in its fullness. It was a path of humility—a going down to the ground of who we are. Adam, who had been alienated from the earth by trying to transcend it, is answered in Christ the transcendent one who goes down toward the humus, bending to wash feet and heal beggars and spit in mud to give sight.

We can't choose our ancestors. Mostly, we can't choose our inheritance. But we can decide, even if imperfectly, what to do with them. We can look to new models, and find new families born of water rather than blood, baptism rather than genetics. But that refiguring takes death, and a *no* to our past; it takes going down before we can go up.

What will my children, those who come after me, inherit here? The agrarian writer Gene Logsdon writes that, "If your gravestone could read, 'Here lies a person who left his land with over 5 percent organic matter in it,' you could rest assured that you had contributed as much good to the earth as any famed scientist, philosopher, or philanthropist. Maybe more."[1] I have no hopes for a headstone, but I long for such a eulogy. And so I compost, I gather leaves from neighbors curbs, I work to renew the life of this place.

My children will inherit something from me, my family, the community of this place and beyond. They have received the common ancestry of us all, in Adam and the *adamah*. In receiving these inheritances, they will gain both gift and curse. What wisdom and care we can give will be passed on and from it they will find their own path of love. But they will be burdened too, by the debts of our ignorance, or more so our hubris. And so I teach them forgiveness, for we cannot live without it, and we cannot accept our ancestors unless we practice it. I'm sure that I will need it from them and from all those who will inherit what I've left behind.

---

1. Logsdon, *Gardener's Guide*, 3.

Dirt

In our backyard, suspended from an old climbing rope slung over the branch of a tree, we have a swing. My daughters love to lie in it, the motion lulling them into a calm as they sing or talk or tell stories to the wind. I like the swing because, though they sometimes play together or with friends, they most often swing by themselves. The swing provides a place beneath the open sky, surrounded by the whir of bugs, for them to be alone with their thoughts and imaginations.

The swing, however, has caused a problem. The constant dragging and pushing of their feet has worn away the grass beneath it and left the soil bare. This summer we've gone for weeks without rain and the bare spot has become dusty, little plumes of earth rising in the wind. We are losing a patch of topsoil.

The problem of this patch of earth beneath the swing is a problem played out on a much larger scale in this state and country and world. I recently drove through the eastern part of Arkansas where acres of soybean and cotton fields stretch for miles. There were plumes of dirty air sweeping into dust devils, tiny tornados of soil spinning across eroding fields. These fields were bare of vegetation, recently plowed for the next crop in the rotation. And with so little rain there was nothing to keep the earth in place.

What I was witnessing along that road, what is happening beneath the swing in my backyard, is a loss of soil. It is a crisis that doesn't tend to make the news, but it is as critical as any war, far more than the latest political entertainments from Washington. For generations now we have been losing the rich earth from which we can grow good crops. Chemical fertilizers have been a Band-Aid that has helped cover the wound. But without real healing, the disease has begun to fester, and even the bandage cannot hide the sickness beneath.[1]

1. See Montgomery, *Growing a Revolution*, 49

DIRT

Geologists make a distinction between soil and dirt. Soil is the kind of earth that will grow something. It is by its nature alive. The better the soil, the more alive it is. In contrast to soil, geologists offer "dirt." Dirt is the basic physical and chemical stuff of the ground, but without life. Dirt can't really grow anything (at least not without major, continuing inputs of chemicals) and what might grow from it will be unhealthy and prone to disease. Dirt is dead and as such can offer no life.

The ancient people who wrote and assembled what we call the Bible were people who knew about soil and dirt and the difference between the two. As an agrarian and pastoral people, they had a land-based language and vocabulary. So it was that they had a word for the living and life-giving soil, the arable land—*adamah*. This was the kind of ground that is good for growing crops—generative earth. It is from this soil that the human being is formed.

Then there is the word *apar*. *Apar* is the top layer of the earth, the crust of the *adamah*. And though some new translations have called it the "topsoil," it has been more traditionally translated "dust." This older translation indicates the ephemeral nature of the *apar*. Disconnected from the networks of life, *apar* is like that dust whipped up in the winds of East Arkansas—the devastating storms of dust that marked the Great Plains states in the era of the Great Depression.

Soil, rich in organic matter and living creatures, is literally glued together. Discovered in 1996, glomalin is a substance created by mycorrhizal fungi that binds clods of earth together. This glue, along with the other glues produced by bacteria, help create the "crumb" structure of good soil. They also help to prevent erosion. When agricultural systems such as tillage, however, break up those life systems, little or none of those glues are produced and the earth easily erodes away—soil is turned to dirt, *adamah* becomes *apar*.

The ancient people of Israel may not have known of glomalin, at least by that name, but they knew that dirt could turn to soil and soil to dirt and that the difference lay in relationship. All life in the biblical view depends on God's breath. To live, as animal-being, breathing-life was to share in God's breath, and no soil could be generative without God's sustaining presence. Death is being cut off from that breath. As Psalm 104 puts it, when God withdraws his breath, creatures "return to their dust," their *apar*. Dust is what we are apart from the relational life of God—it is the common and raw material from which God creates and gives life.

"In a place naturally whole, everything is living," writes Wendell Berry. "As long as the Wheel of Life turns in place, undiminished and uninterrupted, death is alien; nothing is 'dead' that is not already transforming into new life." Such is the life of the *adamah*, the soil, the world inhaling and exhaling God's sustaining breath.

"Insofar as the nature of a place is fragmented," Berry goes on, "the balance is thrown over in favor of death, of what we call 'waste.'"[2] And so it is with life removed from the cycles of creation, the land mined rather than cultivated becomes dead and turns to dust, whipped up in the wind—a breath that goes forth and does not return.

---

2. Berry, *Art of Loading Brush*, 194.

Till and Keep?

Green and yellow, its flowers long like drooping tentacles, laden with seed, it can grow two to three inches a day—almost animal in its speed. It is the stuff of nightmares, at least for those farmers who must worry about its impact—millions of dollars in lost crops, 80 percent of a harvest. The plant is a "super-weed," increasingly immune to whatever chemicals drench the fields, frustrating hopes to interrupt its return.

Palmer Amaranth is a native of the southern United States, loving the hot and humid delta where it thrives in open spaces. A relative of spinach, its leaves are nutritious and have been eaten for generations—a cure for scurvy and other diseases of malnutrition. High in protein, the seeds can be ground to flour or cooked like rice. They pop like popcorn when heated in a skillet, which is how the native people of Latin America ate its far South cousin.

For the world of row-crop agriculture this remarkable plant is hardly a gift. It is an angel of devastation that easily overshadows the cash crops in the ground. It has driven bankruptcies and lost farms, murders and suicides. Nuisance, noxious, pest—none of these adjectives seem right to describe it. Curse is a better word, a biblical word, for Palmer Amaranth is a kind of plague. But like the plagues of the Bible, cause and effect are complex, symptom and disease must be sorted out. Palmer Amaranth is no more the problem than swarms of locusts or the blood-red Nile—it is a sign, a witness of something gone wrong.

The wrong is ancient, reaching back to the rise of agriculture. "Farming is humanity's original sin. We, not the devil, eroded the ecological capital of the soil," says the ecologist Wes Jackson. To put a plough into the ground, to till it, is to begin a process of disruption that undoes creation. A plough is a dangerous tool, a weapon of violence. Swords into ploughshares, no thank you (a broadfork or hori hori would be better). The ground should not bear the blade any more than a person should. Wes Jackson writes from Kansas, where in the nineteenth century a plough designed by John Deere made possible the movement of pioneers into the West. It was called the "Prairie Breaker," and the violence of its name is appropriate to what it wrought in the landscape.

I've seen a handful of native prairies. Grasses and forbs, perennial flowers and small shrubs. Together they build a tight weave of protection over the ground, the soil blanketed by the patchwork of plants. Birds make their homes there, controlling insects, gleaning seeds from flower stalks and then spreading them in fertilized droppings. There is a rhythm of fire and grazing, dying grasses turned to compost for new growth.

There is an integrity to a prairie. It has a cohesion, a melding together of life in balance. The blaze of a wildfire, the scream of a mouse in the talons of a harrier. These are moments in a wholeness that contains them. There is a kind of rest in that completeness that marks any true household of life, any ecosystem that has settled into a harmony.

The ancient story of Eden reflects that restfulness, a foundational peace at the heart of the world. "The LORD God took the man [*adam*] and put him in the garden of Eden to till it and keep it" (Gen 2:15). So goes the story after the humus-being was given life breath. It's a short line, but like most things in the Bible, there is a lot happening in those few words.

Yanach is the word for "put" or "placed." But according to the biblical scholar Kristin Swenson, the word "bears the sense of rest, repose, quiet."[1] What work there was, was not labor. It did not break the quiet, like the domineering noise of engines, but added to the humming song of life. There were no prairie breakers in Eden.

And yet we're told that the *adam* was placed in the garden to till it. If, as Jackson says, agriculture is our true original sin, how should we read this call to till? Perhaps that is what the poet had in mind, but as with any good poetry, the meanings play with a multitude of possibilities—different ways to hear the text.

Avad can be "till" or "work," as it is usually translated, but it could just as well be read as "serve." The human was placed in the garden to serve and keep it. This last possibility offers us a different way into the call of the human. At its best, *avad* is a word that connotes cultivation rather than

1. Swenson, "Care and Keeping East of Eden," 376.

TILL AND KEEP?

control, tending rather than violence. This vocation of service is further clarified by its pairing with *shamar* as the two-part vocation of the *adam*. *Shamar* means to keep, to preserve. It puts a form and so a limit on what might be done. To keep the garden is to tend to its integrity, to ensure the ongoing flourishing of its life. Our *avad*, our work of service must be toward that end of preserving. "The human being was rested in the garden of Eden to serve and preserve it." That is the vocation of the *adam*, but it was a call that was misunderstood as human life moved east of Eden. Our vocation was not so much lost, as altered. We came to hear *avad* as tilling without service, plowing without keeping. And the response of the earth was to protect itself against this violence. The ground cursed by human abuse responded with thorns and thistles, weeds to resist our careless cultivation.

※

"Cursed is the ground because of you; in toil you shall eat of it all the days of your life;" says the LORD God, aggrieved by the human violation of Eden's limits. "Thorns and thistle it shall bring forth for you; and you shall eat the plants of the field."

We have heard this story many times, and we usually take it as an explanation for why work is hard, why farming continues to be a challenge despite the best efforts of our industry. But perhaps there is another way to hear the lesson of this story and our situation. Maybe we shouldn't see thorns and thistles, or Palmer Amaranth, as mere curses but as correctives, a protective limit. What if weeds are not inevitable, but are rather a call to work (*avad*) within the patterns of keeping (*shamar*)?

※

Let us say what a weed is. A weed is any plant that is an obstacle for human intentions in a landscape. This definition works for thistles, and it works for Palmer Amaranth; it could also go for dandelions and Japanese Honeysuckle. By itself a weed is just a plant doing what plants do—growing in the little niche of creation for which they are suited. Some are native plants with a long history in a place, like Palmer Amaranth. Others, like Japanese Honeysuckle are introduced species that have become invasive. A plant becomes a weed when it gets in the way of another vision for that landscape— a garden, a lawn, a nature preserve, or a five thousand acre soybean field. Whatever their kind, a weed always carries with it a message, something to which we would do well to listen.

My own introduction to hearing weeds came from a small yellow paperback with double-stapled binding. The cover had an illustration of a green dandelion, mustard, and plantain with the title in a handwritten script popular in the 1970s: *Weeds and What They Tell* by Ehrenfried Pfeiffer (later republished as *Weeds and What They Tell Us*).

Pfeiffer was a German soil scientist and one of the pioneers of biodynamic agriculture. The book, written in the 1950s, explores a variety of common weeds and what to do about them. But unlike the industrial approach that seeks to know weeds only to find the appropriate poison, Pfeiffer was interested in understanding their ecological function in the soil. Weeds, more often than not, are plants with a particular role in building soil and healing it. "They are witness of man's failure to master the soil," wrote Pfeiffer, " . . . they only indicate our errors and Nature's corrections."[2] They show up, not to be a reminder of our suffering in a post-Eden world, but to play a role in restoring the landscape, to remind us of where we went wrong.

Palmer Amaranth, or "pigweed" as it is colloquially known, is such a plant. It likes disturbed soils and industrial agriculture has given it plenty of them. The ground, when not planted in a crop, is usually laid bare—easily eroded by wind and rain. Each season, following the long-established practice, farmers disk and plow the fields—turning under the stubble and forming the land again into long furrows. Much of this process is done for the sake of machines that make quick work of the landscape: tilling, planting the crop, and applying just the right amounts of fertilizers and pesticides.

Ecologically, these fields are in need of healing, and plants like Palmer Amaranth are the agents of creation that begin that work, the early succession plants that help build the soil and restore it. When the ground is disturbed, tilled and laid bare of any vegetation, it is wounded. Amaranth is a kind of emergency response, quickly able to take over a field. It doesn't need much nutrition to grow quickly, and like Dandelions it has a deep and strong tap root that can help break up compacted soil. In a natural system, Amaranth would eventually give way to other plants as the quality of soil changed and the ground was no longer disturbed. With industrial row-crop agriculture, however, that disturbance continues. And there is no end in sight, unless we learn listen to this weed and what it has to say.

---

2. Pfeiffer, *Weeds and What They Tell*, 10.

Till and Keep?

In the Arkansas Delta two brothers have begun to listen. Adam and Seth Chappell were farming 8,000 acres of row crops and spending $100 an acre on herbicide to kill Palmer Amaranth. The herbicide wasn't working and at such an expense it wouldn't take long for them to go bankrupt. Instead of giving up, however, they began to think differently about the problem. They heard what the Amaranth was telling them: to keep the soil intact and work toward its health. And they responded to that call, moving to a no-till system, leaving the residue of harvested crops, planting cover crops, and engaging in other soil building activities. They worked to prevent the disease that the Amaranth was coming in to heal and as a result, Palmer Amaranth is no longer a problem and neither is the erosion of the soil.[3]

Our relationship with the creation needs healing. Perhaps it is a matter of our work within it, our *avad*, being separated from the call to keep, *shamar*. If we keep both together, listening to the land and serving it, then we will find no other way to live into the call to "till and keep" other than to not till and thus preserve the life of the soil we were called to serve.

---

3. Raylene Nickel, "Palmer Amaranth Opened the Door to Cover Crops and No-Till on Arkansas Farm," *Successful Farming*, November 26, 2018, https://www.agriculture.com/crops/cover-crops/palmer-amaranth-opened-the-door-to-cover-crops-and-no-till-on-arkansas-farm.

Scything and Reaping

In his reflection on the traditional farming life in the Lake District of England, James Rebanks describes his family's long struggle with thistles. As a boy, Rebanks would join his father and grandfather, cutting back thistles using scythe, sickle, and tractor. "Thistles were one of nature's ways of taking our land back, making farming hopeless," writes Rebanks.[1] The fields that were stony and too steep for tractors were a particular challenge. They would labor, hacking at the thistles as swifts flew overhead catching the fleeing insects and goldfinches perched on the purple flowers whose seeds they gladly ate and spread.

It was difficult and endless work, a constant contest. Rebanks thought, as a boy, that they were like Sisyphus—cutting the thistles only to have them grow back again. But from his grandfather he learned that this regular rhythm of labor was a kind of grace—a way of entering the basic and blessed work of provision for their family and the land. "My grandfather seemed to have found a way to endure it through enjoying the wild things around him, and in doing things right," says Rebanks. "He seemed to be saying to me: learn to see the beauty in mowing thistles, learn to enjoy the skill of the scythe, learn to tell stories or make people laugh so that even the toughest working days won't break you." In a life of such labor, Rebanks's grandfather "thought, harshly, that modern people were like children, free to play, but bereft of meaning in their lives and disconnected from the things that mattered."[2]

To scythe a field, year after year to clear it of thistles, is hard labor. It could be called futile, like Sisyphus and his stone. This is life east of Eden, bread by "the sweat of your face" (Gen 3:19). But in response to this hard path of resistance, Rebanks's grandfather is an example of the long line of

1. Rebanks, *Pastoral Song*, 56.
2. Rebanks, *Pastoral Song*, 89–90.

those who responded by finding an Eden in the rhythms of the world, listening hard for its reality beneath the din. The writer L. M. Sacasas has called this "the path of grace," one "marked by humility and gratitude. It is the path of grace precisely as the etymology of the word grace suggests, it is the way of the gift. It is the way of those who are prepared to be surprised, who have resisted the temptations to plan, manage and control their circumstances."[3]

The other path is the way of control, a rejection of the conditions of creaturely life with its limits and labors. This is the promise of industrial agriculture with its chemicals and machines, and as Rebanks grew up his family was tempted into its promise against mounting economic pressures. As fewer people were around to work on the farm and neighbors were increasingly turning to "modern" methods, Rebanks's father, though initially resistant, decided to deal with thistles the chemical way. He sprayed an unruly field with herbicide.

The result was stunning. "Work that had taken three of us several days every summer no longer needed doing," recounts Rebanks. "Our fields started to look much tidier, and more like the neat modern farms we knew . . . The spray was bloody miraculous stuff."[4] It would take years before Rebanks would begin to realize that all of the natural world that had delighted and kept his grandfather going was also disappearing. The more they controlled the landscape, the less life was shared with hedgehogs and swifts, curlews and goldfinches. Rebanks, thankfully, found another way, but all too often the story of our world has followed the other path—the way of violence set by our ancestor Cain.

The story of the world's first murder begins with brothers, one a shepherd and the other a farmer. Even as a child, it had always seemed to me that Abel would be the more capable killer. He kept sheep, after all, animals meant to be killed. Like David after him, Abel also likely had more than a few contests with wild beasts. A vegetable farmer, on the other hand, seems anemic, not the sort that would go around bashing heads in. Fighting off potato beetles and hornworms probably didn't give Cain any skills in cutting throats. But maybe the violence here is more fundamental. Maybe it

---

3. Sacasas, "Resisting the Spirit of Babel."
4. Rebanks, *Pastoral Song*, 115.

is violence against the *adamah* that starts the chain that leads to killing another *adam*.

The narrative, like so much of the "primeval" history of the Scriptures is both thin and textured. Like a Zen koan, we're left with empty spaces to fill in. So it is that both Cain and Abel bring a sacrifice to God: Cain's, the produce of the field and Abel's, the produce of his flocks. Genesis tells us that God looked favorably on Abel's sacrifice but not on Cain's. No reason is given, exactly. We're left to wonder why and my wondering leads me to the soil.

Abel is a "keeper of flocks," the story tells us. Though the word in Hebrew is different from the call to "keep" (*shamar*) given to Adam in Eden, there may be something analogous in Abel's role. To keep sheep is a kind of dance between the wild and domestic. Especially in traditional shepherding cultures, like Rebanks's "fell farm" in England, the sheep are often quite on their own. The role of the shepherd is one of protection and tending, but not one of complete control. Like a permaculture farmer, the shepherd is one who creates a frame and then lets the work of creation go on within it, intervening here and there only when necessary.

This is quite different from tillage agriculture. In these systems, labor is intensive. One must constantly work the ground, and because such a working disrupts the natural patterns, it requires ongoing management. What if the favor of God toward Abel's sacrifice and rejection of Cain's is due to the different forms of agriculture in which they were engaged—Abel a keeper, Cain a violent exploiter? Israel, though it engaged in grain agriculture, would always prize shepherds over farmers. There may have been something in the mythos of the people when these stories were first told that helped form this orientation—an ideal rooted in what the landscape needed and a response to the grain-based empire of Babylon in which they were captive. We can only wonder.

The surer ground of interpreting this story comes in what happens because of God's response to Cain's sacrifice. Cain is dejected and God sees where such resentment will lead, warning that "sin is waiting at the door ready to strike" (4:6 CEB). But rather than following God's call to "have power" over the sin, Cain overpowers his brother and kills him. Abel's blood is swallowed by the *adamah*. Like a medium possessed by another's soul, the earth receives Abel's life and speaks on his behalf, condemning Cain before God. As biblical scholar Mari Joerstad remarks, "It is as if Abel and the ground have become one being. The ground opens its mouth and takes Abel's blood, and Abel, in response, uses the mouth of the ground to cry out to God."[5]

When God hears this cry from the earth, he asks Cain about his brother. His response is telling. He asks if he is to be his brother's keeper? The word keeper here is *shamar*, the same word used in the Edenic vocation to serve and preserve the garden. Abel's blood is crying out from the very soil that Cain has been working in denial of his call to preserve it. Now that violence has extended to his brother Abel, the human and the humus connected in a intertwined nexus of mutual life.

The curse that God then gives Cain is that he will be separated from the ground. The earth here is no passive background, but is instead an active agent, a creature choosing to cooperate with the ends of God rather than Cain. It is because of this that the earth will resist Cain. Cain who has engaged in the tilling of the earth, interpreting that call as one of working rather than serving, will now be alienated from it. The soil, now filled with blood, will refuse to cooperate. But what does Cain do in response to this curse? He flees from the presence of God and builds a city in a restless place, a land called "Wandering."

---

5. Joerstad, "Ground That Opened Its Mouth," 710

The Restless City

In the morning we sit on the porch, a wide concrete slab, two faux wicker chairs and a small table between us. There is a swing at the end of the porch and just beyond it a massive elderberry, growing from a swale. Before us stands a bed of blackberries, another elderberry, a pawpaw, and a volunteer oak we are letting grow as it pleases. Birds feast at the feeders, scavenge among the leaves and brush. There are half a dozen species at any one time, sometimes more.

This is coffee time—a moment at the beginning of our day when Emily and I sit, unpack dreams, talk through ideas, greet what comes. We start early, usually as the light is breaking in the east, but even so there is always a background hum, the interstate not far away. The morning traffic has already started and will grow ever louder until the crescendo just before nine, cars whirring to work and school according to the clock schedule of the machine. We will join them, eventually, despite our best efforts, contributing to the noise, but for now we sit, resting, a moment of sabbath grace in what we are trying to make as a refuge.

The rush of metal and machine, impatiently moving toward some aimless end, has always represented the city to me. There is no quiet here, always there is a hum and roar. Not long ago I was walking along a country road, a remote place in the mountains of Arkansas, and I was overwhelmed by the silence of it. For a moment, before a jet buzzed overhead, I could hear no engines, no machine sounds, and I realized that it had been a long while since I had experienced such silence. Sound and silence, rest and restlessness—these contrasts are at the heart of the options for how we should live.

❧

I've been reading Jacques Ellul's *The Meaning of the City*, a used copy, hardbound. Reading may be too passive a term for how I've engaged with this book, pencil in hand, inserting brackets and stars and exclamation marks in the margins. This is a book whose lines invite engagement and leave a reader changed. Here's an example of a line, marked off in graphite, starred in the margins. Just after Ellul notes that Cain flees from the presence of God's protection after the curse, he writes, "And now Cain will spend his life trying to find security, struggling against hostile forces, dominating men and nature, taking guarantees that are within his reach, guarantees that *appear* to him to be genuine, but which in fact protect him from nothing."[1]

Here's another: "Cain has built a city. For God's Eden he substitutes his own, for the goal given to his life by God, he substitutes a goal chosen by himself—just as he substituted his own security for God's. Such is the act by which Cain takes his destiny on his own shoulders, refusing the hand of God in his life. And if someone thinks I am drawing unwarranted conclusions, let him remember that this city is called Enoch."[2]

Enoch is a name rooted in the Hebrew term for "initiation" or "dedication." For Ellul, this represents an opposition: "Inauguration, as opposed to creation. Initiation, as opposed to the garden paradise. The city as opposed to Eden."[3] Cain, the tiller and worker of the ground, who refused to understand his vocation as service and denied his call to keep, now becomes the inventor, the creator, the builder. In opposition to the original call of the human to serve and preserve the creation, mastery now replaces service, innovation replaces preservation.

Inventor, maker, builder—the vocations of Cain are now the basic career plan of the successful. Everyone wants to become an innovator now. Our heroes are entrepreneurs and disrupters. Even in the world of the market, to be the successful founder of a startup has more cachet than the executive of a "legacy" company. Our education systems are geared toward the disciplines of innovation—science, technology, engineering, math, with a sometime nod to art. What is missing—history, philosophy, literature—all those reflective disciplines by which we might look at our frenetic movement and wonder—why?

On the porch, we wonder why. It's a moment of rest, the kind of space that feels like a place in Eden—the Sabbath at the base of the world. We have

1. Ellul, *Meaning of the City*, 3.
2. Ellul, *Meaning of the City*, 5.
3. Ellul, *Meaning of the City*, 6.

been cultivating this space. Most of the plants here did not just spring from the ground. But we are not its builders, either. We are more hosts than creators, welcoming and working with a process already at play. I formed the swale, digging a trench and piling up the dirt, but I did so according to the contours—lining out the shape of the yard with an A-frame and a fishing weight to determine the slight slope of the ground. I planted the blackberries, but in a place where the sun and earth were suited for them. I am always asking, how can we welcome more life here? What is it that this place wants to be? The work is a participation in what is already happening—the grace of the world.

Drawing on Ellul, L. M. Sacasas writes that: "[W]hat Cain managed to do by choosing the path of technological mastery, by refusing the postlapsarian human condition, was to hide the face of God from himself. He turns away from the hope of grace to the expectation of human self-determination and ingenuity."[4] And so by refusing the way of grace, Cain is trapped in a frantic life that will never settle into a place or identity. Rather than being a creature, conditioned by the particular givens, the unique graces, of a human life, Cain and all his children are unable to ever settle. Though Cain founds a city, it is not a true "settlement," it is not a home where life can be enjoyed as it has been offered.

Pascal, writing early in the modern era, remarks, "What people want is not the easy peaceful life that allows us to think of our unhappy condition . . . but the agitation that takes our mind off it and diverts it. That is why we prefer the hunt to the capture." Cain settles in the land of Nod, the land of wandering, and so avoids facing the truth of who he is as a creature. But there is another impulse within us, a way of grace that Pascal says may offer us some freedom in the truth of who we are. "[People] have another instinct, left over from the greatness of our original nature, telling them that the only true happiness lies in rest and not in excitement."[5] The challenge is to not deceive ourselves about this rest, to recognize that it is available now, even in our work, not after some impossible finish. This work, to be restful, must learn to live and labor in the rhythms that are the peace of the world.

---

4. Sacasas, "Resisting the Spirit of Babel."
5. Pascal, *Pensees*, 40.

The Place of Love

Several years ago the novelist Jonathan Franzen offered the commencement address at Kenyon College. He began by talking about his new Blackberry, which at the time was the latest and greatest PDA—"Personal Digital Assistant." In reflecting on this device and how it responded ever more obediently to his every whim, Franzen found an insight into the end game of technology: "[T]he ultimate goal of technology, the telos of techne, is to replace a natural world that's indifferent to our wishes—a world of hurricanes and hardships and breakable hearts, a world of resistance—with a world so responsive to our wishes as to be, effectively, a mere extension of the self." The telos of techne, in other words, is Cain's dream of escaping the limits of creaturely life, the reality of life east of Eden.

Franzen went on to suggest "that the world of techno-consumerism is therefore troubled by real love, and that it has no choice but to trouble love in turn." To live so that the world is completely bent to our every whim, responsive without frustration to all of our desires, may give us the simulation of the freedom our Enlightenment forebears so longed for, but it cannot help us love an authentically other person, someone who, by the reality of their independence, is free from our own desires.

"Humility is, above all, a respect for the nature of things," writes Australian monastic Michael Casey, "a reluctance to force reality to conform to subjective factors in ourselves."[1] Humility, then, is a way toward love. It helps us to enter the world, the real world that resists our desires to shape it according to our wills. Real love is always built in a relationship with an other that is not ours to posses or mold. To love God, my spouse, my children or my friends, is to love those whose lives are independent of me. In my love, I come to adore them in their otherness. That love ends as soon as I try to manipulate them into the mold of my own desires. What we share

---

1. Casey, *Guide to Living in the Truth*, 18.

together is always a middle between our subjectivities—a sharing that is not either person's will or vision alone.

Apathy, it has been said, is the opposite of love and this seems especially true in the realm of digital life. In apathy we no longer care for the other; we don't long for the reality of relationship that is beyond our subjectivity. Boredom is the problem digital technology promises to solve, but boredom is a problem, ultimately of our care. If I am bored with something, it is because it does not meet my expectations. And yet, it is by working through boredom that transformation of the self can come. This is why simply sitting in silence and time spent in solitude are part of most traditions of self-transcendence. To be bored is a valley of attending through which we must journey toward a more selfless self. Yet escaping boredom is what the restless world in the lineage of Cain, which is now represented by much digital technology, is aimed toward.

To counter the temptations of the virtual, we must learn to be bored, to endure it and the temptation to rid ourselves of it. Many of the great spiritual masters, from St. John of the Cross on down to Dom Chapman, wrote of the need to encounter a "night of the senses" that would enable one to move into new realms of contemplative experience. Such a night is a time when the old forms no longer work and the life of prayer is no longer exciting. Here is where growth happens, like the roots of a plant making their winter journey, descending through the cold earth in order to be ready for the rapid growth when the sun returns. To learn to endure boredom of the right kind is an essential aspect of what it means to be human.

So often I am bored because such and such a thing or event does not stimulate me. The problem is not with the world, but with myself—it is there that the work must be done. But responsive technologies, such as Franzen's Blackberry or my "smart" phone or whatever the latest product's "augmented reality" offers, are designed to liberate me from that inner work. Play a "mindless" game, scroll through pictures, read the flitting "news" to feel that one is well informed about the world—all of these are distractions that keep us from the hard encounter with reality, especially as Franzen says, the reality that may hurt us, that may make us suffer.

Quoting his friend Alice Sebold who talks about "getting down in the pit and loving somebody," Franzen writes that, "She has in mind the dirt that love inevitably splatters on the mirror of our self-regard." This dirt, the humus of humility, breaks us out of the ether of the ego and puts us into the real community of creation where everything is not made for our delight and yet everything is created as good.

"Taste and see that the Lord is good," the psalmist said. To learn to taste and see goodness involves a kind of cultivation of the senses. Part of growing up is learning to appreciate what is truly good apart from the simple satisfaction of our preferences. One of the functions of a working culture is to help a person to appreciate goods that are not immediately apparent. Children may not like spinach, but their dislike says more about them than it does about the vegetable. If their eating culture is good, then eventually they will learn to enjoy leafy greens and even seek them out. There are limits to such cultural work, of course, but still it is essential. It is through the work of culture that one learns to blend the self with the world, to turn outward from the ego and look with expectation, curiosity, and wonder at the world beyond.

"Love is about bottomless empathy, born out of the heart's revelation that another person is every bit as real as you are," Franzen writes. "And this is why love, as I understand it, is always specific. Trying to love all of humanity may be a worthy endeavor, but, in a funny way, it keeps the focus on the self, on the self's own moral or spiritual well-being. Whereas, to love a specific person, and to identify with his or her struggles and joys as if they were your own, you have to surrender some of your self."[2]

Love, then, is for the particular, the unique places and creatures of the world. We are not God and thus we cannot, in the words of the famed verse John 3:16, "love the whole cosmos." Our loves, like our lives and bodies and very spirits, are limited. Which is why fidelity is key in the Christian ethics of love. It is to say that we can only really learn love in its depths through the encounter with this particular other. That a move toward "polyamory" is apparently rising in our culture is not a result of an expanded circle of "many loves" but is instead an outgrowth of consumerist selves unable to dwell in the particulars of a single beloved.

Couples who have long lived into a good marriage often speak of the continued discovery of the other. The depths of another are endless, the realities never fixed. To be in a loving relationship with another demands that we always encounter them with an openness, a stance of listening. Otherwise we

---

2. Jonathan Franzen, "Liking Is for Cowards. Go for What Hurts," editorial, *The New York Times*, May 28, 2011, https://www.nytimes.com/2011/05/29/opinion/29franzen.html.

will just subsume their life into our own. Without a watchful wonder present in our encounter with another, whether person or place, we will devour that other into the mirrored pool into which we will eventually fall and drown.

Just before writing this I looked out the front window of my house. I had been on a digital meeting with colleagues. I needed to get up and outside. We have some flowers growing in my front yard, perennials that were planted by the people who owned this house just prior to us. Each summer they bloom a mix of yellow, orange, and pink. Both hummingbirds and butterflies feed on them, and though the flower is not a species native to this place, it has been a window through which I can glimpse an aspect of life here—the varied creatures that can be lost from view for their smallness.

Today as I glanced out the window, I caught a glimpse of a large skipper butterfly with a protruding forked tail. Though I'd never seen one before, I knew immediately that it was a long-tailed skipper, a butterfly whose normal range is hundreds of miles south of here. I ran quickly to get my camera to document the butterfly, photographing it for several minutes. Through the magnification of the lens I could see the turquoise green of its body, clearly reflected in the light, the long elegant protrusion of its tail. The skipper was beautiful and completely unaware of its rareness, perhaps even of its beauty (though butterflies can see spectrums of light and color invisible to the human eye). This was simply a butterfly being a butterfly, living its life in the common household relationships of flowers and insects. It cared nothing for me and yet I could not help caring for it, loving it even in a desire for its life to be good and full.

This is the kind of love that will help save us. It is the limited, finite expression of human love for the particular through which we can learn to embrace certain people and animals and places. From such love we will find what is needed to work for their survival and flourishing. It was this lesson that helped Jonathan Franzen move from the anger and apathy in his youthful environmentalism. He stopped caring about the "environment," and became concerned instead for the plight of the particular birds he came to love. "My love of birds became a portal to an important, less self-centered part of myself that I'd never even known existed. Instead of continuing to drift forward through my life as a global citizen, liking and disliking and withholding my commitment for some later date, I was forced to confront a self that I had to either straight-up accept or flat-out reject." Franzen was freed from the operations of the ego and was opened to an encounter with the real and living world.

Franzen found love by encountering the particular—an encounter that humbled him. Love is complemented by humility and must be grounded in it. Love is desire and reaching forth, but we must have a place from which to offer its gift. Humility gives us a place to stand; roots from which we can reach for our beloved without being knocked over by the embrace.

Powers and Repentance

In *The World Beyond Your Head*, the philosopher Matthew Crawford offers a deep look at Mickey Mouse. In the old Mickey Mouse cartoons, argues Crawford, all of the comedy came from an encounter between the self and a world that did not yield to our choices. The world, in these early cartoons was an independent force that refused to obey our will. As Crawford puts it, "These early cartoons present a rich phenomenology of what it is like to be an embodied agent in a world of artifacts and inexorable physical laws."[1] That's where the humor of the old cartoons came from—slapstick stories of folly and failure in the face of a world with a mind of its own.

Crawford contrasts these older cartoons with the new "Mickey Mouse Clubhouse" on the Disney Channel. There, "The Clubhouse is filled with amazing technology that always works perfectly," writes Crawford. "There is never any insoluble problem, that is, a deep conflict between the will and the world."[2] All anyone has to do is say, "Oh, Toodles" and suddenly the solution presents itself. This is the ideology of the solutionists. "Innovation," "STEM," "Silicon Valley"—they are our "Toodles." "This cartoon magic may be fanciful," writes Crawford, "but one would be hard-pressed to find any meaningful distinction between it and the utopian vision by which Silicon Valley is actively reshaping our world."[3] In that vision, all we have to do is call and technology will solve everything for us, even death—our own or the world's.

The promise of solutions preys on the inherent optimism of the human mind. There seems to be something deep within us that holds out hope for some ingenious tool that will solve our problems. It is this reality that makes so much internet click-bait work: "Try this one weird trick for

1. Crawford, *World Beyond Your Head*, 70.
2. Crawford, *World Beyond Your Head*, 72.
3. Crawford, *World Beyond Your Head*, 72.

better health," "Do this one easy exercise for perfect abs." We know, usually, that it can't be so simple and yet we still want to find out, we still imagine that somehow the perfect solution is out there, easy and unexpected.

This optimism protects us from the hard work of adjusting our lives to the reality of both truth and goodness. This is at the heart of the human dilemma because we have always been environment-altering creatures. We are not alone in this, many creatures from fire-spreading birds to forest-farming fungi create habitats that suit them. The problem is that in every case in the given world there is a balance and resistance. It is a question of power and the limits to that power. Our limits are legion, but we've become better and better at externalizing or extending the effects so that we don't feel them—at least on the individual and collective level of the present where most of our choices are made. The world gets hotter and we get air conditioners, the oceans rise and the rich move to hilltops, fossil fuels become problematic and so we start mining rare-earth minerals and lithium to keep the industrial economy going through "clean energy" (a term of newspeak, if ever these was one).

The one-weird-trick mentality is not limited to technological solutions either. I've seen more than a few upbeat documentaries promising that our ecological woes will be solved if we just stopped eating meat or we unleashed the power of soil health to capture carbon. These documentaries are based on a mathematical optimism that is calculated in carbon counts. And while I think a mass conversion to soil health practices beautiful and hope-filled, they are not going to "solve" the problem of our ecocidal economy and culture. We cannot heal the world by reducing carbon emissions; it can only be healed by dealing with our rebellion against the given lives of our humanity.

Wendell Berry put this point stridently in a commencement address he gave at the College of the Atlantic, where he told the graduating class that: "The religion and the environmentalism of the highly industrialized countries are at bottom a sham, because they make it their business to fight against something that they do not really wish to destroy. We all live by robbing nature, but our standard of living demands that the robbery shall continue . . . We must achieve the character and acquire the skills to live much poorer than we do."[4] This is the old advice of the great spiritual traditions of the world—we don't learn to live anew while burdened with the excesses of our lives as they are. When we have become comfortable by means of theft

---

4. Berry, *What Are People For?*, 201.

and avarice, having less is the only way by which we can return again to the gifts of the given world.

In her book, *The Story of More*, the ecologist Hope Jahren offers a similar take: there is no answer to our problems other than to live with less. She doesn't mean the pop minimalism of bloggers or television shows about tiny homes, but rather the hard truth that our economies and standards of living have simply outgrown the capacity of shared, diverse life on the Earth. Reflecting on the nineteenth-century economist Henry George, she writes, "most of the want and suffering that we see in our world today originates not from Earth's inability to provide but from our inability to share. It is because so many of us consume far beyond our needs that a great many more of us are left with almost nothing."[5]

Our voracious appetite for more cannot be solved, she says, by solar panels or wind power or any trick save a withdrawal from the *more* of our lives. This is a hard truth because it requires hard work. "Even if you consider yourself on the right side of environmental issues and a true believer in climate change, chances are that you are actively degrading the earth as much as, or more than, the people you argue with," writes Jahren. "An effort tempered by humility will go much further than one armored with righteousness."[6]

In the forests near my house, I am always fascinated to see a fallen tree, its roots exposed. I look through the tangled subterranean arms, now surfaced, and I get some picture of what is always beneath me in the forest floor. In healthy forests, however, an uprooted tree is not common. The roots of the varied trees interweave and hold together, anchoring themselves in the ground. Our work, in an age that looks toward ever greater heights, is to deepen our roots, entangling our lives with the networks that will hold us in place. To do this, we must, as Jahren and Berry call us, learn to live on smaller scales, leading lives that make room for greater sharing, the entanglements that sustain us. This work should not be done as one more solution, one more "weird trick" that will solve the problems of ecocide. We must instead learn to see the failure of our denial, the ashes of our efforts,

5. Jahren, *Story of More*, 14.
6. Jahren, *Story of More*, 170–71.

and stop making it all worse through our continued attempts at solutions. Before we can offer any healing, we should turn toward repentance.

In the biblical stories of repentance, such as the dramatic turn of Nineveh in the book of Jonah, repentance is marked by fasting, sackcloth, and ashes. This work is the work of ceasing, a withdrawal from the normal realities of life. In sackcloth and ashes we lament, we face the reality of our deaths, and we go near to the ground. In fasting we interrupt the normal flows of life, the normal patterns by which we live by consuming. In this ceasing, our normal lives are arrested enough that our perspective is changed—we are snapped, for a moment, from the reflexive realities of our lives. In the end, this mourning turns to joy, as the true nature of our turning shows us that we were on the wrong path and have been graciously, if difficultly, turned around.

And yet such a repentance is hard to keep. The demand of the normal is a gravity so strong that even wars and pandemics rarely shake it. Early in the SARS-CoV-2 pandemic the general feeling was of change, that things will never be the same again. The streets were quiet, people in large cities heard birdsong they'd never experienced before, and there was a sense of strange newness to the world.

We wake to the new morning, but what will we do with the day? All too often we fall back into our normal patterns. The pull of the normal is strong and automatic. As Bill McKibben wrote in the *New York Review of Books*, "most of the momentum destroying our Earth is hardwired into the systems that run it."[7] The same is true of racism, whose automatic nature is what makes it so tractable and powerful, always changing, never going away until it is finally faced in its fullness.

There is, then, much talk of changing the systems. We imagine that if we could just change the systems then the turning around of repentance will be possible. But that again goes back to what T. S. Eliot said, that we are trying to make it so that we don't have to be good anymore. We find ourselves locked between the work of each of us and the work of all of us. The biblical language of "Powers" is a helpful concept that can enable us to better understand this tension, and how we should live in response.

---

7. Bill McKibben, "130 Degrees," *The New York Review of Books*, August 20, 2020 https://www.nybooks.com/articles/2020/08/20/climate-emergency-130-degrees/.

In the letter to the Colossians, written by Paul or some person in his camp, the author speaks of Christ defeating the "Powers." The Powers are created and yet intangible realities—elements of earthly life that have participated in the rebellion against God and must be brought under subjection to Christ's reign. Perhaps the easiest way to understand the nature of these "Powers" is to think about how the economy works in our world. The economy is a power. We talk about it in almost personal terms, as though it is a reality with clear agency. We speak of what is good for the economy. We talk about the market solving this or that problem. The economy has preferences, likes and dislikes, it confers its favor on certain people and institutions and not on others. It must be obeyed or our collective well-being will not be possible.

Economies and markets are not bad things. They are natural outgrowths of the exchanges of energy and matter, relationship and craft, that are fundamental to the creaturely life. But "The Economy" is a Power in rebellion—a created reality that has become more than it was ever meant to be and stands outside of the control of any earthly being. Presidents cower before The Economy and will never make a decision to violate its wishes. This Power's priests, the agents of the market, seek to appease its wishes, but can never fully tame it. The Economy serves its own ends and is no longer a tool for the flourishing of creaturely life. That is why "market" solutions always fail to protect the vulnerable realities of our world, be they Cerulean Warblers or human children—The Economy is a rebellious Power and as such is aimed, ultimately, at the annihilation of the creature. It cannot be healed on its own terms.

It may sound here like I'm speaking of something demonic, and in a way I am, but not in the sense of a personal Satan manipulating the Economy like an evil puppeteer. The anti-creational forces of annihilation are often more subtle in their operation. The Economy as a rebellious power is in many ways automatic in its actions. Like the worst nightmares of Artificial Intelligence, it is just following the program, but it is a program out of order—a musician in a symphony playing her line without hearing the other musicians or paying attention to the conductor any more.

Hannah Arendt, observing the trial of the Adolf Eichmann, architect of so many of the atrocities of the Holocaust, noticed the pure normality of his evil: "The trouble with Eichmann was precisely that so many were like him, and that the many were neither perverted nor sadistic, that they were, and still are, terribly and terrifyingly normal. From the viewpoint of our legal institutions and of our moral standards of judgment, this normality was much more terrifying than all the atrocities put together."[8]

The problem with Eichmann, and the problem with so many of us, is that we have given ourselves over to a life of systems and abstract powers that carry us along. We participate in them without thinking what we are doing. This, Arendt believed, was at the heart of the operation of evil. As Amos Elon explains in his introduction to Arendt: "Evil comes from a failure to think. It defies thought for as soon as thought tries to engage itself with evil and examine the premises and principles from which it originates, it is frustrated because it finds nothing there. That is the banality of evil."[9] Ours is a time of no thinking. We are enamored with our devices and the increasing power of Artificial Intelligence, but there is no widespread attempt at artificial thought. This is because thought is not important to the advancing powers and likely it is impossible for anything but a living creature. Thought does not serve the advance of the machine. The recovery of thought is among our most critical tasks and it requires grounding our lives in the sphere of the properly human.

To return to the human is the work that Christ came to do. It is in becoming human against the distortions of pride and shame that Christ defeated the powers. He accomplishes this defeat, not through some heavenly invasion, riding down in flaming glory with the Four Horsemen of the Apocalypse. Instead, it is through a subversion that begins with a disavowal of power. Christ overcomes evil by humbling himself, going down to the humus and showing us what it means to be human once again. It is a path of humiliation.

8. Arendt, *Eichmann*, 276.
9. Elon, "Introduction," xiv.

Humility

Can't nothing bother me when I have my hands in dirt. It's like I'm talking to God with my fingers.

JESMYN WARD, *SING UNBURIED SING*

Humility does not rest, in final count, upon bafflement and discouragement and self-disgust at our shabby lives, a brow-beaten, dog-slinking attitude. It rests upon the disclosure of the consummate wonder of God, upon finding that only God counts, that all our own self-originated intentions are works of straw. And so in lowly humility we must stick close to the Root and count our own powers as nothing except as they are enslaved in His power.

THOMAS KELLY, *A TESTAMENT TO DEVOTION*.

. . . humility cannot be humiliated.

HOWARD THURMAN, *JESUS AND THE DISINHERITED*

Anaerobic

In a corner of my backyard, there is a pile of black dirt. When I press a pitchfork into it, the soil breaks into sticky clumps, almost like tar, and inside I can see rice hulls, a carbon source I added early in the spring, still intact seven months later. Recently the pile has been buzzing with green scarab beetles who, I assume, are laying egg that will one day become the grubs my daughters love to dig and hold, their white wriggling bodies like subterranean caterpillars.

This pile of dirt is a humiliation, a failure. It represents months of work gone bad. I did not, at first, understand the failure or even that I had failed. The pile seemed to be functioning just fine, transforming coffee grounds and vegetables scraps into soil. But at some point, as I added more coffee grounds than wood chips, more sweet potato peels than rice hulls, the smell went bad and each turn of the pile revealed slick rot more than humus forming. Eventually I came to learn that the pile had gone anaerobic, all the wrong kinds of microbes going to work. They have their place in the work of decay, yes, but in soil meant to aid the growth of plants they offer few benefits and many problems.

For one, they release greenhouse gases such as methane rather than binding CO_2 to the silts and clays of dirt. In addition, these anaerobic microbes exude alcohols that dissolve the roots of plants. I've seen them do their work in compacted soils. Pull up a tuber planted in a soil dominated by anaerobic microbes, and it will be a slimy mess rather than a plump potato. While I had set out to create a "hot pile," an energetic mix of decay that hosted aerobic microbes and fungi, the makers of humus, I had ended up with an anaerobic failure, cold and useless unless healed.

Compost is concrete and complex. It is not some magic formula, easily responding to the desires of a gardener. Compost is a fickle reality that requires both art and science. It works or it fails and because of that it is an opportunity for humility for it will surely, at one time or another, deliver humiliation.

To be humiliated requires something of us, it is not simply something that happens to us. For those on the side of power, humiliation can be grounding. But for it to serve that purpose, we need a readiness to recognize and admit our failures, to embrace the grounding they bring. Those who are captive to pride do not admit their mistakes and so whatever inevitable error they have committed does not deliver the gift of humiliation to them. They are people who never ask for forgiveness because they think they have never done anything wrong. It takes a kind of arrogance to think in this way, but there are many people who have stood at the pinnacle of our public life who possess such pride, some might even consider it a political virtue.

The more subtle problems, though, are the ways that pride operates as a system of human life. Systems are webs in which we become entangled, spaces where individual virtue is challenged and compromised by the power of the collective. Our collective system of pride hinges on our attempt to engineer goodness, to make it so that our goodness no longer relies on our virtue, individual or collective. Harm reduction becomes the reigning paradigm, a system ensured by formal rules rather than lived morality.

We often escape humiliation by living into realities that insulate us from it. Like the gnostic dreams of a pure spirit, freed from the "weight" of bodies, the smell of shit, we create technologies and systems that protect us from the experiences of concrete failure and thus the opportunity for humiliation.

In his helpful book, *The World Beyond Your Head*, the philosopher Matthew Crawford writes about the importance of practices that enable us to concretely engage with a world that resists us. Crawford writes that certain philosophical strains born from the Enlightenment project have changed our conception of the self into a reality that is primarily formed through the freedom to choose:

> According to the prevailing notion, to be free means to be free to satisfy one's preferences . . . Reason is in the service of this freedom, in a purely instrumental way; it is a person's capacity to calculate the best means to satisfy his ends. About the ends themselves we are to maintain a principled silence, out of respect for the autonomy of the individual. To do otherwise would be to risk lapsing into paternalism. Thus does liberal agnosticism about the human good line up with the market ideal of "choice." We invoke

the latter as a content-free meta-good that bathes every actual choice made in the softly egalitarian, flattering light of autonomy.[1]

Such a conception, Crawford believes, shields the critical mind from the ways that our preferences are in fact constantly manipulated. We are largely defenseless as long as we keep ourselves chained to the technological realities that protect us from the free exercise of our will. What Crawford offers in response is a call to encounter the world "beyond your head," that is, the world that exists with little interest in your preferences and certainly doesn't seek to cater to them. This is the world where compost piles go anaerobic, the ground is never level, and an attempt at growing something is met with ever novel challenges. This is the world, in other words, of finite creatures who are plagued with ignorance and impotence, the world of fully human lives.

Ignorance and impotence are the facts of our lives, but it is only through humility that we can properly live into their reality. Otherwise we find ourselves rebelling at every turn and that rebellion leads us, inevitably, to a denial of reality. Pride could, in fact, be defined as a denial of reality for it is both a rejection of what has been given and a refusal to recognize our givenness, the world, and our place within the whole.

The German Catholic theologian Dietrich von Hildebrand defined Satanic pride (clearly the worst kind) as a "value-blindness" in which the prideful person is so interested in his own excellence that "he is unable to grab the inherent beauty and nobility of objective values."[2] This person "would fain be 'like God'" but he does so by embracing power rather than goodness. "He shuts his eyes to the goodness and holiness of God," writes von Hildebrand, "he fails to perceive the indissoluble union between all-powerfulness and all goodness; he would separate omnipotence from all-goodness and attribute the former to himself."[3]

Against this pride we can only hope for a jolting failure through concrete realities of creatureliness. These are the humiliations that can heal. All too often, however, following the way of Cain, those wrapped in pride and power turn toward the humiliation of others. It is this form of humiliation that humility defends against, for it is a true grounding in the truth against the illusions of the powerful. As Howard Thurman puts it in his book *Jesus and the Disinherited*, speaking of Jesus's teachings on

1. Crawford, *World Beyond*, 18.
2. Von Hildebrand, *Humility*, 9.
3. Von Hildebrand, *Humility*, 9.

humility in the face of Roman oppression: "Natural humiliation was hurting and burning. The balm for that burning humiliation was humility. For humility cannot be humiliated . . . . Thus [Jesus] asked his people to learn from him, 'For I am meek and lowly in heart; and ye shall find rest unto your souls. For my yoke is easy, and my burden is light.'"[4] So grounded in the humus, the humble have a place to stand. It is from that place that roots can run beneath the surface and the power of the powerless can grow against the illusions of the age.

---

4. Thurman, *Jesus and the Disinherited*, 17.

Compost and Contemplation

In the fall, I cruise my neighborhood, scouting my next steal. A good house is one that has plenty of tree cover and no dogs. The best time to make the actual run is on a Thursday morning, the day before the city comes by to collect yard waste. Most people aren't home at that time, so I don't feel strange driving up to their houses, jumping out of my car and tossing their trash bags in the back of my hatchback. It feels a bit thrilling, but of course anything on the curb is fair game. It's not my problem that they are trashing their treasure.

What I want are the leaves. I avoid maples, not wanting to chance the toxic Norway species that will kill other plants around it. Oak and hickory are best. A few pine needles can be tolerated, though they tend to be acidic—best used as mulch for blueberries and azaleas. Leaves are free fertility, the carbon needed for my compost piles, the rich mulch that will provide a feast for the worms that turn the soil, excreting beneficial microbes that will add to the diverse life beneath my garden beds.

To compost transforms what was once just waste—an indistinguishable collection of refuse all headed to the landfill, now becomes a resource, something so valuable that if you really get into it, the meager offerings from your own kitchen and yard simply aren't enough. When that happens, you start to collect other people's trash.

For me, that has meant not only snatching bags of leaves, but also carrying buckets of coffee grounds down the street, hauled once a week from my neighborhood coffee shop. At first I felt like I should be paying them, but the baristas soon made it clear that I was lightening the load of their end-of-shift trash. In exchange they gave me free espresso drinks whenever I came by, so, in addition to nitrogen rich grounds I also gained free premium coffee. The same hasn't quite worked out yet with the beer mash I sometimes collect from a local brewer, but we'll see.

Composting, I have found, is more a way of life than a garden activity. It transforms how I see the world and interact with it. Everything becomes potential soil—a "green" or a "brown," a source of carbon or nitrogen to be mixed in the ratio that will heat the pile and turn it to a rich humus, fragrant like a forest floor.

Shredded paper, cardboard boxes, table scraps, manure, urine, distillery grains—the list could go on. Nearly every artifact of organic life is a potential source for new soil. To become that soil, though, it must all be brought together in the right ratios and allowed to transform into the new stuff of living humus.

In this way, compost can be a form of prayer, or a living metaphor for it. It is a spiritual discipline that, like fasting, is useful for its own ends but even more so as a means of entering a new relationship with the energies of the world.

The Augustinian monk and teacher Martin Laird writes that "Like compost, prayer breaks down into fertile matter for the life around it. Prayer matures by a process of breaking down rather than by acquisition and spiritual prowess."[1] To allow prayer to break down requires humility and waiting. It takes welcoming even the discarded and the dead into the potential for new life. As Laird writes elsewhere, "What gardener condemns the compost for being full of rubbish?"[2] So it is with the life of prayer, indeed the life of faith. We take it all in, the good and the bad, and we let it settle and mix and be transformed by the invisible life that works always in and around us.

The virtue that is required for this work to take place is humility, the rejection of power and prowess in favor of a going down and letting go to discover again the truly human form. "[T]rue humility," writes Laird, "is the wide open space of self-knowledge that opens onto God."[3] Essential to that self-knowledge is an acknowledgment of our mortality. For compost to become humus, death must be involved. And for us to become humble, renewing and recovering the art of creaturely life, death will inevitably be a part of that too. The best prayer, like the best composting, is that which enters the truth of that death and is released to the Life that sustains through it and beyond it. This is the life of a creature made and sustained by God,

---

1. Laird, *Sunlit Absence*, 90.
2. Laird, *Into the Silent Land*, 126.
3. Laird, *Into the Silent Land*, 127.

a creature who has abandoned all to the "perfect humility" that is the "unfathomable love of God, who is the ground of our being."[4]

---

4. Laird, *Into the Silent Land*, 128.

The Death of a Ewe

The first compost pile I ever made was not for vegetable scraps but for bodies. I was an apprentice farmer at the time, and I was learning how to raise sheep. One of the first lessons of that apprenticeship was that sheep die. They get old, they get sick, they get slaughtered by coyotes and people, lambs are stillborn, summer rains and warm weather overwhelm old ewes with parasites—the ways are varied but at the end there is always a body.

When I began working at this farm, the dead were incinerated. There was a makeshift pyre behind the barn where wood would be stacked, and a flamethrower was used to start a blazing fire. It was effective but not efficient. Incineration, at least as we were doing it, required a lot of inputs in time and energy, and since that time and energy were mostly mine (being the apprentice) I began to look for an easier way.

In one of the many farming journals I was reading at that time, I came across a story about a composter who had begun to take whole cows and horses—turning them quickly into dirt. In other places, roadkill were being effectively turned to soil. If a cow could be composted, I thought, surely a sheep could.

Composting of any kind begins with the mixing of carbon and nitrogen. In the right combination these serve as food for a whole host of microbes—bacteria and protozoa, nematodes and fungi who set to work transforming the mix into soil. It is the basic process of decay that will happen naturally, but the process is accelerated by creating the optimal conditions for a quick return to soil—millennia turning to months.

Natural humus formation is a slow process of accrual—nature is in no hurry. Composting is a kind of useful shortcut, quickly speeding the process to several weeks with the right recipe and work. Carbon is the critical food, the basic building material of both soil and life, but when mixed with just the right amount of nitrogen, the metabolic process of decay

The Death of a Ewe

accelerates and a well-formed compost pile can get so hot amid the frenzy of life that it bursts into flame.

After trial, and much error, we were able to compost the animals that died on the farm. And with time, we returned them to the soil to grow the bodies of new sheep, lambs suckling grass-fed milk, ewes feasting on clover and fescue. It was a beautiful cycle of life to death to life again. We had taken an extractive and expensive solution to a problem and had found a way to do things in closer keeping with nature's way and pace.

There was one night, early in those days of composting, that the farmer I apprenticed with was out of town and his daughter, J., was in charge of putting the sheep in the fold. It was mid-summer and there had just been a rain. The air hung thick and humid, a warm fog.

As the sheep came in the count was off. J. walked the fields and not far from the pond she found an old ewe, laying on her side, her legs stiff with rigor mortis. It was getting dark; the time coyotes would begin their loping. A dead ewe was an easy meal, but once attracted, they would likely turn to the living sheep in the fold. She couldn't wait until morning to move the body.

Moving a large ewe is a difficult, two-person job, so she called me to come help. I met her by the barn, and we rode together through the pasture, jostled by the terrain, the occasional hard bump of a woodchuck hole.

The body was already a buffet by the time we came to it—orange and black carrion beetles, flies of iridescent green, maggots bursting from around the eyes and other soft tissued places where their small mandibles could begin to tear. If we had left her there, and the coyotes and vultures had begun their work, there would have been little more than hair, bones, and a few sinews within a day. This ewe who had lived her life from the grass would become it again, CO_2 and sunlight mixed with minerals from the ground below, feeding next spring's lambs. All flesh is grass, proclaimed the prophet Isaiah. This ewe would confirm the ancient truth.

Resisting our reflexes at her stench, we dragged the body around the back of the truck. I took hold of the fore legs, J. the back, and with a 1-2-3 heave we lifted the ewe into the truck bed, spreading her body on a frayed blue tarp.

The compost pile we were using at the time was on another plot of land, a couple of miles down the road. The ding and clang of gravel beneath the truck gave way to the smooth whir of the blacktop. There was a low fog hanging over the pavement, the rain evaporating from the sunbaked road.

As we made our way, I said that I found something beautiful in the abundant life that had gathered around the ewe's body—the way life always sprang from death. J. and I were both Christians, schooled in a theology that saw death as something to overcome, death as a reality born of the rupture between God and creation that we call "The Fall." That death could be beautiful, even a source of life, seemed somehow a heresy to us at that time. But seeing the ewe, I couldn't help but wonder, what if death is even a part of paradise? What if it is one of the essential realities and gifts of being a creature?

I raised the question with J., and she countered that most deaths on the farm were not those of old ewes. Most deaths were lambs convulsed by the toxins of bacterial blooms, sheep killed in their prime by coyotes whose methods were merciless, the wasting away of an animal plagued by intestinal worms. Could that be good?

We talked, as I pressed a pitchfork into the hay and wood chips, digging an opening deep into the compost pile. Steam rose from it, the metabolic burn of microbial life already heating the core of the pile, ready to transform this ewe into earth. We talked of Eden and all that lay east of it. We reflected on the incarnation and the resurrection. We talked of suffering and hope. And like most such talks, we left with more questions than answers, neither convinced wholly of the other's side. They are questions that have stayed with me; questions that return every time I turn a compost pile and wonder at its beauty. I ask, is this decay feeding new life not the resurrection already at play in the world? To see death as an aberration and suffering as evil is to see so much of creation as a tragedy when even the death, even the suffering, can burn with beauty and wholeness. What if lions eating lambs are as much a part of the paradise to come as lions lying down beside them?

The Shadow of Death

The test of our compost piles were always the coyotes. Raccoons and opossums, vultures and foxes—there were plenty of other scavengers about, but it was the coyotes who were most likely to smell a rotting body beneath the wood chips and dig it out. We learned, with trial and error, how deep to bury the dead. A good pile was one where no smell would hint at what was hidden beneath, and we eventually became quite good at creating that.

Coyotes have been a wild shadow for much of my life. I grew up in rural places in Arkansas and Texas, and we would see coyotes from time to time, usually at a distance against the edge of the woods or along a fence row. Lope is the right word for their movement; they travel with a lazy trot. And though the coyotes always avoided us, they carried in their bodies a kind of insolence—a reminder that they were leaving by preference and not fear.

Once, when I was in a back pasture tending to my pigs, a coyote ran past me carrying one of my chickens in its mouth. It was a daring move in daylight. I sat the next few evenings waiting with a gun, but only got off a warning shot or two. The longer I farmed the more I came to prefer animals like pigs and cows that weren't the easy prey of these long-legged dogs. And yet, now that I live well away from a rural place, I'm always thrilled to see a coyote in a wooded park or forest edge. Despite the damage they wrought, I could see in these coyotes a kind of kinship.

Humans live, like coyotes, from the death of others. We've abstracted the process, removed ourselves from the mess of blood and entrails, the plucking of feathers and skinning of flesh, but still we live from what has died. This is true, in many ways, even of those who avoid eating meat. Many an animal has died to bring forth a plate of tofu. Harvesting soybeans often kills rodents and birds in the process and any farmer is an avid enemy of insect pests. No meal is free of bloodshed and killing.

I have killed animals and seen them killed in ways that do not haunt me. To take the life of an animal should be a sacred act—one that recognizes the sacrifice and the gift of living from the life of another. When I raised sheep, we would often sell a lamb or two for the Eid holidays. A group of Muslim men would come to the farm, and we would provide a place where they could kill and clean the lamb according to their faith. I would be nearby and hear their prayers before the skilled cut of the knife, the lamb's life quickly spilling as blood to the soil.

The most direct experience I have had with killing was when I raised chickens for a season. Unlike cattle, sheep, and pigs, the Department of Agriculture allows chickens to be butchered and sold directly from a farm in small quantities. With the help of some friends, I was involved in slitting their necks, plucking their feathers, removing the warm mess of their organs from inside. There's something profound about the experience of witnessing the death of the animal that feeds us. It is a part of being human, following the creaturely pattern of our omnivorous bodies. And at our best, it is not all that one-sided after all. We too are meat for something, be it bacteria or the scavenging vultures that tilt above my yard every day. Still, in killing an animal, there is something that resists within us. I talked with a hunter recently who said that the older he gets, the more deer he lets walk on by his stand. A kill, even a good one, contains within it something tragic. Can death be both good and evil? And how do we discern the differences in that mix?

Karl Barth helped me begin an answer, a yes and a no (and perhaps a maybe). Barth was a Swiss theologian who worked in the pulpit and the classroom through the twentieth century's most hideous wars. When facing the rise of Nazism, Barth served as the primary author of the Barmen Declaration—the theological statement of independence by the "Confessing Church" that refused to cooperate with the Nazi state. He understood the loss inherent in limit and lack, pain and suffering. He understood the monstrosity of evil as it played in history and the place that death occupies for such evil. And yet he didn't see death, in and of itself, as evil. Death, he argued, was a part of being a finite creature; it was not evil but an aspect of creation's shadow-side. "Light exists as well as shadow, there is a positive as well as a negative aspect of creation and creaturely occurrence," he wrote.[1]

This shadow, for Barth, was not a flaw in creation. To have light means that we will also have shadows: "It belongs to the essence of creaturely

---

1. Barth, *Church Dogmatics* III.3, 295.

nature and is indeed a mark of its perfection, that it has in fact this negative side, that it inclines not only to the right hand but also to the left, that it is thus simultaneously worthy of its Creator and yet dependent on Him . . . ."[2] "Perfection" because to be a creature is to be finite, to be limited, to get old and sick, to die—in these things we do not betray our being but live into its reality. We are, as the old and wise word designated us—mortals. Our death is no accident but an essential aspect of being a creature. Along with ignorance, lack, and limit, it is a part of who we are. Without those things we wouldn't be creatures, we wouldn't be part of that blessed reality God made and called good.

This shadow side of creation, however, is easily confused with another force at play in the cosmos. This power is what Barth calls the Nothing. The Nothing is that adversarial reality that seeks the annihilation of the creature. In death we are still creatures, we remain in relationship and dependence upon God, and so we can welcome the new life that God brings. But when we enter the Nothing our very creatureliness is destroyed—we are drawn into the void. It is the Nothing that stands against God; it is, as Barth goes on to say, "the break in the relationship between Creator and creature."[3]

Rowan Williams, the former Archbishop of Canterbury, has noted that within the human person there seems to be a "deeply rooted aversion to our own creatureliness."[4] It is Nothingness that tempts this aversion. We want to be free of our creatureliness and so we seek to rupture the relationship of dependence upon God that defines creaturely life. The result, of course, is not our liberation but our annihilation. We are creatures all the way down, and when we deny that, we cease to be. In a way then our very opposition to the creaturely reality of death can be a temptation toward Nothingness.

"HELPED are those who lose their fear of death; theirs is the power to envision the future in a blade of grass," writes Alice Walker, riffing on the Beatitudes.[5] This bit of gospel from Walker's fictional character Shug Avery, reflects the proper attitude of creaturely life. It is against this acceptance of death and limit that we find the impulse of Cain, the temptation to heal the wounds of our finitude by transcending them. It is following that impulse that leads us into the rupture with creation and our Creator. From it flows not life or transcendence, but every form of exploitation and violence.

2. Barth, *Church Dogmatics* III.3, 296.
3. Barth, *Church Dogmatics* III.3, 296.
4. Williams, *On Christian Theology*, 77.
5. Walker, *Temple*, 336.

The terror of death, the smallness of insignificance, the worry of lack and limit and starvation—these are the things that have driven the embrace of the Nothing in our world. From the killing fields of Cambodia to the latest innovations of "transhumanism," we seek a way out of our shadows, and in so doing ally ourselves with an even darker reality (albeit one that appears to be light). We don't want to risk being creatures; we don't want to trust that God will hold us through all the limits and pains of our lives or remember us in our deaths and so we move like moths to the flame of nothingness out of fear of the shadows.

The Death and Nothingness we should stand against is not a death born of finite creatureliness, but our rejection of this dependence, the denial of our limits as mortal creatures. Against this denial, we must learn to be creatures once again. We must learn to live into the truth of our limits and our mortality. That truth is the way of humility, what Fr. Nivard Kinsella has defined as "nothing more or less than the attitude of the creature in the presence of his Creator, and the way of acting which results from such an attitude."[6] This attitude involves an orientation of our gaze—a helpless and dependent looking by which we give up and rest in the love of the Creator.

---

6. Kinsella, *Unprofitable*, 2–3.

Look to You

It could fit easily in my hand, nose pulsing in a nervous twitch, ears bent back across the fur of its neck. My wife and daughters had rescued the rabbit from the mouth of a cat, but as far as we could tell there had been no skin break. It seemed nearly paralyzed by shock more than anything else. My oldest daughter, around five at the time, quickly took up the role of wildlife rehabilitator.

After overcoming her initial shock, the rabbit reacted to our presence with a wild frenzy. She was set on getting away, escaping from these predatory beasts who'd put her in a box. But with time and gentle hands rubbing along her back, the rabbit began to be calm, at ease with our care. By the time we set the rabbit free, back into the wilds of a suburban honeysuckle hedge, she made no attempt at escaping us.

I have seen similar reactions over the years as my family and I have rescued and cared for various wild animals. We've been involved in the rescue of a window-stunned junco, a starving red-tailed hawk, a poisoned gray squirrel. In many of these instances there was a moment when the wild writhing of the animal gave way to a peaceful acquiescence, the raging reactions of fight or flight relaxing into a kind of trust. It was as though the animal realized that we were there to help and submitted to our care. I often think of that transition when I think of the posture of humility, our attitude as creatures in relationship with our creator.

One morning during my sheep farming days, I came to check the animals just as dawn was breaking. There, in the woven fence near the barn, a great horned owl was trapped, talons tangled in the wire. It is not uncommon for owls to meet their end in fences, hidden in the night even to their keen eyes. I've seen dead owls in fences before, but thankfully this one was still alive.

When I approached her, I moved slowly, carefully. I had dealt with injured wild birds before, but never a raptor like this. Her talons were fierce and her beak a bladed edge that could easily have sliced my skin. But the whole time I worked to untangle her, after what I'm sure was a whole night of struggle, she looked at me through the perfect circles of her yellow eyes—steady and acquiescent. In her look I could sense a kind of trust. I was her only hope of getting free, and she seemed to have accepted that.

To fully be a creature is to live with that gaze of helpless trust. This does not mean that we cannot live our free and wild lives. Instead, even in our freedom, we must recognize that we are dependent, that every moment of our lives is a gift and a grace. Our freedom is fragile, our lives tenuous. Humility is the gaze of trusting dependence that recognizes that we need help to live in our fullness, to achieve our wholeness.

In the great creation song of Psalm 104 there is an image of this gaze. After naming the span of creatures from flocks to cedars, from birds and human beings to the sea monster Leviathan, the Psalmist prays:

> These all look to you
> to give them their food in due season;
> when you give to them, they gather it up;
> when you open your hand, they are filled with good things.

In that "look" I think of the helpless gaze of the owl, the same gaze I saw in the eyes of the rabbit and the junco. It is the gaze of helpless acceptance, the recognition that some power beyond us is interested in our good. This is the gaze that I seek in my own heart as I recognize that this is not a world of my making; my life is not my own to do with as I please, but is a gift born of relationship, a gift that needs food in due season and the continued breath of God's spirit to go on living. The psalm continues:

> When you hide your face, they are dismayed;
> when you take away their breath, they die
> and return to their dust.
> When you send forth your spirit, they are created;
> and you renew the face of the ground.

Our lives are like moments in the divine breath, inhale and exhale, carbon and oxygen, death and life. It is by God's breath that we live, it is without God's breath that we die, and yet in this reality we meet a limit, but not our final end. All life is made and maintained within God and God is continually renewing and restoring it.

When we learn to look at God with the dependent gaze of a helpless creature, we accept a posture that transforms even our death. Life in all its difficulties no longer betrays us. Instead, we are able to rest in the world, hoping and yet suffering, living through each moment not as an opportunity for our ambition, but as a gift that we must savor. Our lives become moments between joy and grief. We become a breath inhaled, the body blooming in the red burst of life; a breath exhaled, flesh broken and given to the world.

The Hospitality of Bread

The evening mass was over. The church of stone walls and marble floors, echoed with the footsteps of the faithful as they left. A handful of us, all college students from a nearby Evangelical school, stayed behind at the front. Some of us were part of a reading group of Catholic theology, dubbed by its bearded, long-haired leader: "The Dead Fathers Society." Several had converted or were actively in the process of becoming Roman Catholic. Others, like myself, were more curious, along for the ride.

The priest of the parish was clearly excited when we came up afterwards to introduce ourselves. A group of Evangelical college students would be a win for the church, I'm sure. But instead of selling us on the virtues of Catholicism, he offered what I took to be a strange act of hospitality—he invited us to a side chapel to spend some time in adoration. In my limited experience with Catholic worship, I didn't know what adoration was. But when we entered the chapel, before us in the darkened room, there was an object on the altar that looked like the corona of an eclipsed sun. Enclosed at its center, the object crowned by blazing rays of bronze, was a small piece of bread.

Host is the technical term of the church for this bread. It is the bread of communion that offers hospitality to Jesus Christ who is somehow present in it. To sit before this piece of bread, to look at it with a loving gaze, is to dwell with that mystery. To eat the bread in a service of Eucharist is to join with creation in our own bodies to offer hospitality to the Creator. In this mystery Christ plays host to us and we to Christ, creation and Creator in a call and response of shared song.

Somewhere else in the church I'm sure there was a crucifix. The Roman Catholic Church is known for its love of this symbol, one that outsiders often take for an obsession with suffering. On the crucifix, there is not only the cross, but the body of Christ hanging on it—his head low, his side pierced. He is dying or dead.

"God is dead, God is dead, and we have killed him," cried Nietzsche's madman. That was no news to the faithful, for the death of God is at the center of our faith. It is by God's death that we are offered the broken body of Christ; it is by death that we receive the hospitality we then offer in return through the communion of all creation.

A good death like a good life is always hospitable. It is made full and flourishing, not by an independent existence, but through the web of common life. Our bodies are not our own, and they cannot survive on their own. We are always made of other creatures, dependent upon them and they on us. To separate ourselves from them, as so many of us attempt to do in our sanitized world, is to enter into a kind of living death. In this "death" we keep our lives to ourselves and for ourselves rather than joining in the feast of all creation made of giving and receiving.

The bread of the Host requires death. "I assure you that unless a grain of wheat falls into the earth and dies, it can only be a single seed. But if it dies, it bears much fruit," Jesus taught his disciples as he prepared for his own death. And so it is with the fruit itself, for the dead seed that goes into the earth is also the seed milled into the bread of life. All creation, if it is alive, is involved in the cycle of this gift.

This is especially true of the networks of life in the soil that are made possible by a grand exchange of offer and reception. Plants offer the metabolites of sunlight in the form of sugars to the bacteria of the soil. These bacteria fulfill various functions for the plant, but most importantly they turn nitrogen into forms that the plant can use. To get these forms of nitrogen, however, the bacteria have to die—some through the natural cycle of their life, others by being the prey of protozoa and nematodes that then excrete the rich remains into the soil.

This is only the lowest level of life—microbes and the plants they help grow. But all through the cascade of life's energy, the flow science calls the "trophic cascade," death and eating are essential. It is in death that we finally release ourselves to the banquet of our connections; it is in death that we become a part of the common body of the earth.

Christ offering himself to the world to the point of death was an act of great humility. *Tapeinos* the Greeks called it: lowliness, being close to the ground. The source of the word in Greek is uncertain. But in English it is clear enough—to be humble is to be close to the earth. It is from that closeness that life and growth are made possible. A seed suspended away from soil is just a dead complex of matter, but when it falls to the ground it becomes a life because it is joined to the great communion of life.

Death is the condition for the feast, the possibility of life. In eating the bread of Christ, in gazing upon it, we are witnessing the truth Jesus taught—it is by death that we are welcomed into the meal, it is by death that the hospitality of bread is made possible.

Humility is necessary for this hospitality. The Host of Christ's body, around which the feast of the Christian meal is gathered, is the humble reality of dead seed grown in soil made from the dead material of leaves and lives, all transformed into the humus. It is a sacramental reality that reflects the death that Christ endured in order to welcome the abundant communion of all those who have eaten from the table of Christ's feast.

Those people, the ones we call members of the Communion of the Saints, have received the hospitality of bread, and they in turn offer it to the world. But in that offering, they too must join their lives in the death by which bread is made. They too must learn the truth that there is no life without death. Training into that death is at the center of Christian existence; it is a truth we remember with fasting and ashes.

Ash Wednesday

In the best case they are the fronds from Palm Sunday, burned to carbon black. I've been in churches where this takes place in the midst of the Mardi Gras celebration, cake and booze flowing while we prepare the sign of our death in a February fire. The ashes are never burned all the way to white dust. The fronds become char, an oxygen depleted blackness whose remaining carbon forms a skeleton of what it was.

The priest holds her hand out in a sign of consecration, the ashes in small bowls upon the altar:

> *Almighty God, you have created us out of the dust of the earth: Grant that these ashes may be to us a sign of our mortality and penitence, that we may remember that it is only by your gracious gift that we are given everlasting life, through Jesus Christ our Savior. Amen.*

This ash, the burned remains of living plants, is like the char that the native peoples of the Amazon made, covering smoldering pits of leaves and sticks with soil, creating a black mass of carbon that can turn acid soil neutral and provide the structure that allows abundant life to thrive.

The Portuguese colonialists called it *terra preta de Indio*—"black soil of the Indian." It is known now as "biochar," a potential way to draw excess carbon dioxide into the soil, all the while enriching the biology of the ground. Whatever hope lies in that use, the native peoples of the Amazon had it right—ash can be a source of life.

Nutrient leaching is a problem in the soils of the tropics. With the high level of rainfall and warm temperatures, organic matter is metabolized quickly, vaporized into gaseous forms that leave the soil depleted of the nutrients

HUMILITY

needed for crops. Through biochar, however, nutrients can be secured in the soil, ready to feed plants.

Among the keys to healthy soil is its ability to hold onto nutrients. Soil scientists call this the cation exchange capacity of the soil. Remember your chemistry: an ion is a charged particle, unstable and in need of balance, like a puzzle piece searching for a place to fit. If it is positively charged, then it has more electrons than needed for its balance like the bulbous side of a puzzle piece. If it is negative, then it has fewer like a blank needing to be filled.

Cations are the various soil nutrients that contain an extra electron or two. These ions are seeking balance and so need to bond to negatively charged molecules in order to find balance. This is how soils hold onto the varied nutrients plants need for their growth. A soil with high cation exchange capacity is filled with negative ions that are able to latch on to the positive ions of nutrients like calcium. Soils with a high level of cation exchange capacity have plenty of places to host the molecules of nutrients and make them available to plants. Biochar increases the cation capacity of the soil.

On the biological side, char with its many crevices is like the Kingdom of God, a place of many mansions. Because char has space for bacteria, nematodes, and protozoa to live, there is an abundance of life that is possible in char-rich soil. Each member of the household then works to create an abundance, cultivating the possibility of new life, growth, and then death again. In that process, the life in the soil is able to both connect nutrients to it and to break them free so that plants can use them.

And so it is that ash of the right kind, burned to hold its carbon, inoculated with the life of the soil, can become a possibility for something beyond the death from which it comes. Char can be the household of life's engine, the teeming microbes that made possible the earth's abundant life and sustain it still. From ash we can grow a flourishing garden, a rich diversity of life gathered from what has died before.

I move with the other priests, taking the bowl of ash from the altar to meet the row of people with heads bowed at the rail.

Remember that you are dust, and to dust you shall return.

Ash Wednesday

It is a strange and intimate moment—this smearing of ash. It feels ancient and out of step in all the right ways with a world that is willing to do anything to keep from death. Ash Wednesday is a day about bodies and it is a day about decay, the beginning of a season that moves from life to death to life again.

This is a moment when we remember what it means to be human, living and dying from the earth. It is a time when we recall the view of the ancient peoples of the Bible that by grace, God's sustaining breath, the earth gives life. Left to ourselves, everything becomes ash.

I graze my thumb across the border of the bowl as I smear the ash across the forehead of a woman, well off and well regarded, always dressed in the latest offerings of the boutiques. Some of the black dust trickles onto her nose. Ash is always messy, a betrayal of our best facades.

Remember that you are dust, and to dust you shall return.

Most of us do not touch the foreheads of others. The forehead is an odd space, blaring and public, exposed and vulnerable. Perhaps we will kiss a forehead, particularly of a child, but to touch it, at least in the West, that is left mostly to priests to christen with oil, at baptism or for healing, to bless with a cross tracing thumb, or to smear a sign of life's end in a rude cross.

My youngest daughter was once terrified of ash on her forehead, refusing to go forward, crying when a priest gave her a simple blessing instead. Now, a bit older, she comes forward, looking up expectantly, her blue eyes bright and quiet as she waits.

Remember that you are dust, and to dust you shall return.

To acknowledge the mortality of the old takes no effort, but to remind a child that she will die takes more effort. And yet I know that some will die before I do; that some of these gathered at the rail, so enraptured by the awe of the ceremony, will not survive into adulthood.

Too few of us take the gift of Ash Wednesday to heart. It is hard to practice the ancient art of meditating upon one's death, a practice suggested by the pagan philosophers of the ancient world as much as any Christians. The Stoics have always had a special appeal to the Christian mind, and it is they who suggest that we learn to die in order to live. Yet, even as a global pandemic raged and death was present in ways long forgotten, our anxiety showed that we live in denial, we resist the fact of our end. We have not remembered that we are dust and so we have not embraced the wakeful solace of that truth.

To take the opportunity to accept instruction in our mortality is to learn the ancient cycle of return and to see in it hope for our renewal. Sir Albert Howard, the great British soil scientist, wrote over half a century ago that the disease of our age is "the punishment meted out by Mother Earth for adopting methods of agriculture which are not in accordance with Nature's law of return."[1] We could say "methods of life," for all of our ways of living and dying now deny the return of nutrients to the soil, the body to the earth. We have cut off our bodies and all that sustains them from the nourishing cycles of creation, and so if we are to take Ash Wednesday to heart, if we are to answer its call of remembrance, we must again become present to the truth of our earthly dependence and begin to live, and die, into it.

Remember that you are dust, and to dust you shall return.

After we have been marked with black dust, we kneel, bending our bodies toward the ground. There's a litany of penance, and acknowledgment of our wrongs against God and neighbor. The litany is printed in the Book of Common Prayer, each verse with a pause of silence. It is in the quiet that I add confessions of my own.

> *We have not loved you with our whole heart, and mind, and strength. We have not loved our neighbors as ourselves. We have not forgiven others, as we have been forgiven.*
> *Have mercy on us, Lord.*

We have not honored the laws of return, the gifts of death to life. We have cut ourselves off from the cycles of renewal, we have not let our dust return to dust.

> *We confess to you, Lord, all our past unfaithfulness: the pride, hypocrisy, and impatience of our lives,*
> *We confess to you, Lord.*

We have acted like our own gods, creating our values. We have not honored the creation you called good.

> *For our waste and pollution of your creation, and our lack of concern for those who come after us,*
> *Accept our repentance, Lord.*

Restore us from our brokenness as we restore what we have broken.

---

1. Howard, *Soil and Health*, xxv.

Ash Wednesday

Ash to ash, dust to dust. It is a beginning, not an end.

Every year, in the weeks or months after Ash Wednesday, when the dark smear has been washed from our foreheads and our earthbound lives give way to the ambitions of the everyday, someone will die. Young or old, tragically or in peace, death comes to remind us of our return to soil. And more often than not, even if church was no part of their lives, friends and loved ones will want to mark this transition of their beloved with a ceremony that is sacred.

In the church we gladly say yes, rearranging the week's schedule, going over the liturgy, asking which Scriptures they would like to be read, which hymns they would like to be sung. There are large funerals with full choirs and there are small ones at gravesides. Whatever the circumstance, there is this moment at the end of the service called the commendation. It is a handing over, a letting go of this life we loved or hated and had to deal with in all of the contradictions at the center of every person.

Standing beside the casket or urn, the body or the ashes, the celebrating priest says:

> You only are immortal, the creator and maker of mankind; and we are mortal, formed of the earth, and to earth we shall return. For so did you ordain when you created me, saying, "You are dust, and to dust you shall return." All of us go down to the dust; yet even at the grave we make our song: Alleluia, alleluia, alleluia.

And here is the reality of any human life, caught between joy and grief. We end and yet are held in something greater, a life that encloses ours, even in our death. Held here in this life I can only name as Love, we wait for the Word, the breath that will turn *apar* to *adamah*, ash and dust to the dark, breathing soil of a garden.

Last Wishes

When I die, leave me be. My body has all it needs for its return. Enzymes in my liver and pancreas will let go, and begin their work, digesting my flesh as they once digested food. Leave me as naked as you like, wrap me in a cloth or put me in a basket woven from the branches of the black willows that grow beside the river, where yellow warblers sing their "sweet sweet sweet" in the spring. There will be a feast, I'm sure. The women of the church always have cookies and sandwiches of pimento cheese ready on a platter. Those should satisfy the human guests, but for the others, offer my body as a banquet, a parting gift to the creatures that gave me years of good health. Let them now feed upon the organs inside—coliform, E. coli, streptococci, and Pseudomonas aeruginosa eating up my intestines, clostridia traveling the passages of the body, feeding as they go. May they go into the world, occupying other stomachs, carrying within them a remainder of my body.

Place me in a shallow grave, one where already the dead have turned it dark with life. Smell the place, see if you can push your hand down easily. If it smells like a good garden, the scent of the forest floor like the one I laid on as a child—watching, listening—then that is a good place. If you see the castings of worms, the earth digested in their guts by their own mix of microbes, all the better. Bury me deep enough that the coyotes won't pry, not wanting to trouble the neighbors.

Give at least a few maggots a chance at the softer tissues. They could take care of more than half my body in a week. Beneath the soil, the beetles will also come, especially the burying kind—the grave diggers of the insect world—ripping small bits of flesh and burying it with their eggs, the rotting nursery of another generation.

Eventually, the fungi will take their part. The subterranean decomposers, the great connectors of the soil. They will run their mycelial webs

LAST WISHES

among my remains, searching for nutrients unlocked by feasting microbes and moving them to the ends of the tree roots to which they are fused in a continuous link, a messy tangle—the one and the many. The fungi are as mysterious as ghosts, invisible as a soul, but evident everywhere in the life springing from the ground. They will return my body to that life, the minor resurrection of a human being, earthling brought to life in earth.

When the ground has settled, the mass of my body dissipated in the many-chambered metabolism of the ground, come back to the settled place and plant a tree—something small, a buckeye perhaps. It will bloom red in spring just when the ruby-throated hummingbirds arrive. Imagine my blood in the pigment of the blooms, my body as nectar for the quick beating wings of the birds with gorgets flashing red as they refract the sun. Imagine my flesh as the sweet dew on the uncurled proboscis of the red admiral, settled, leaflike and still.

Dung Beetles

I spotted it, moving along the trail on an old road trace, gullied here and there to reveal the veins of clay beneath the gravel—white with calcium, red with iron. It took a moment to register, but it became clear that this was a beetle, face first to the dirt, its back legs rolling along a small ball. I bent close to look, calling my family to join me. The ball was brown, flecked here and there by the sand it had picked up along the way. It was made from manure, the excrement of some omnivore (at least that's the beetles' preference) that would serve as a place for the insect to lay its eggs or become a snack someday later.

It has been a long while since I'd seen one of these dung beetles. In my days raising livestock they were a common and welcome sight moving through the grasslands. Many ecologists consider them indicator species—a sign of a healthy flow of nutrient cycling. A pasture that is full of dung beetles can keep parasitic nematodes in check because the manure that often contains the worm eggs is being put back in the ground where they can't emerge. Ironically, many de-worming drenches used on sheep and cattle kill dung beetle larvae and so disrupt the natural systems that keep animals healthy.

Dung beetles are not the only beetles that take the waste of the world and bury it. Another family of insects, the silphidae, help return the dead flesh to the ground. The first silphidae I remember seeing was when I was a child, perhaps eight years old, in the backyard of my family's cabin on the edge of an East Texas pine stand.

We'd attempted to nurse a young rabbit to health whose mother had been killed by a mower. The man driving the tractor had brought the rabbit to us, knowing that at times we took such animals and occasionally, if rarely, helped return them to the wild. This rabbit, too young to be weaned, had not made it. So, my brother and I had a funeral—laying the rabbit in the ground, a shoebox for its coffin, dandelions and clovers for its funeral wreath.

After several weeks had passed, however, I became curious. Was there now a skeleton in the soil? What was the state of the decay? I kept a makeshift museum in my room, already populated by fossils, the shards of Caddo stone tools, the skulls I'd found in my explorations in the woods. A rabbit skeleton would be a nice addition, I thought.

I dug down into the shallow soil covering the shoe box and lifted its lid. There was the faint smell of death, the body releasing the chemicals of decay, microbes emitting the gases of varied respirations. Already the eyes were gone, most of the body's soft tissue—the easiest for insects to eat—consumed.

And around the skin, scurrying into and out of the open orifices, were small beetles—orange and black—resembling a flattened bumble bee or a firefly. I cannot trust my memory enough for a proper identification, but they were likely the American carrion beetle or some close kin.

These beetles are often also called burying beetles because they serve as the grave diggers of the natural world, taking the remains of the dead and burying them in the soil. They do this, it is thought, to protect their food from larval flies—the teeming maggots that are quick to appear on any carcass. Whatever the reason, the behavior is an important one for the return of the body to the earth. In burying the dead they are putting the nutrient-rich bodies of animals back into the soil where they can more quickly become the nitrogen-rich material for new growth.

One measure of a healthy ecosystem is how quickly "waste"—manure and bodies, dead trees and fallen leaves—is transformed to soil; how soon it disappears from the place where it fell. In a space of abundant life any scrap of nutrients is consumed, quickly turned into the making of new life, cycling down again into the web of the soil. It takes all kinds—vultures and beetles, coyotes and maggots and the billions of organisms too small to see, too varied to name. Any death is a dance of life and beetles are key among the dancers, pivoting the body beneath the ground, where it will become the stage for another dancer, the food for another movement going up and down upon the earth, like breath—in and out.

A Drain Straight to the Earth

The congregation folded their bulletins, cramming them in pockets or depositing in the blue recycling bins by the door. Hands were shaken, candles put out. Now it was time to clean the dishes. This may seem a simple task, the matter of some water and soap, a dish rag or two. But these were no ordinary dishes—they held the bread of Christ's body and the wine of Christ's blood.

Anglicans don't have an agreed upon theology of how Christ shows up in the bread and wine. We're content with a fuzzy "real presence"—the idea that somehow, in a mysterious way, Christ is present to us in this sacramental meal, offering us grace through the act of eating blessed bread and wine.

Still, in the act of our prayers, we believe this meal is no longer mere bread and wine. It has been sanctified, made holy, and so now it must be treated differently. We cannot simply toss the body of Christ in the trash and pour the blood of Jesus down the drain. Instead, according to the practices of the church, the bread and wine that has been blessed must be either stored for later use in a special place, consumed, or returned to the earth.

In the room, just behind the altar where the dishes are kept, there is a double sink. In most churches that celebrate the sacraments, on one side there is a normal drain, flowing down the pipes to the sewer. On the other, there is a basin called a piscina with a drain called a sacrarium. The drain of the sacrarium does not connect to any sewage system. Instead, it is a drain that goes directly to the earth.

To be a priest, to be religious in all the right ways, is to be constantly aware of the borders of the holy. But as one begins to pay attention to those borders, questions also come. Questions of the definitions of what is in and out. Wittgenstein wrote that it is easier to know what is at the center of a concept than what is at the edges. It is at the borders that conflicts come, exclusion and embrace.

A Drain Straight to the Earth

We say that this bread and wine are holy, and so they must be treated as something sacred. In the wisdom of the tradition, it would not do to flush such holy things down with all the other garbage of wastewater and sewage. To return to the earth, directly, is recognized as the best way to honor the holy.

But thinking about the piscina and its sacrarium that drains to the earth, I can't help but wonder why all drains could not go to the ground? The sacrament of Christ's blood is surely a holy thing, at the center of its definition, but could not shit also be holy? And should it not be returned to the earth in the same way as the bread and the wine of communion? What, after all, of the bread and wine that are consumed? Do we imagine that somehow, they do not end up in the toilet? Is manure not also within the circle of the sacred?

For a gardener, or anyone paying attention to the cycles of earth's fertility, it would be difficult to answer no. My own education in the sacredness of manure began in earnest with Gene Logsdon's book *Holy Shit*. The title, like its author, is both serious and clever. But Logsdon, who once discerned a call to the Catholic priesthood before becoming an agricultural writer, is not calling manure holy in mere jest. He believes that manure is critical to building and maintaining soil health and with it, ecological wholeness. As such, manure has salvific effects.

In his chapter, "How I Came to Find Divine Materials in Manure," Logsdon describes his long fascination with growing Ginseng, an art his neighbor practiced when Logsdon was growing up in the 1930s. This neighbor fertilized his crop with wood soils and manure. It was only decades later when working as a journalist that Logsdon recognized the wisdom of this amendment. Ginseng growers were running into fungal diseases that killed their plants, but research showed that using manure addressed these problems. And this is but one example of how manure, returned to the earth, helps to bring about wholeness and thus health and holiness.[1] It was Logsdon who then introduced me to the work of F. H. King.

F. H. King was a soil scientist who worked in university and government posts in the early part of the twentieth century, including as the USDA chief of the Division of Soil Management. In that role he had a clear view of the growing problems of erosion and soil depletion on American farmland—realities that would culminate in the Dust Bowl of the 1930s. Looking to understand a better way, in 1907 King embarked on a journey

---

1. Logsdon, *Holy Shit*, 141–43.

through Asia. His observations are recorded in what has become a classic of soil ecology: *Farmers of Forty Centuries, Or, Permanent Agriculture in China, Korea and Japan.*

What interested King was how societies that had farmed the same land for hundreds, or even thousands, of years had managed to maintain its abundance. The key word in his title is "Permanent Agriculture." America had had little experience with any long-term cultivation. Through continued expansion to new farmlands, American agriculture had become dependent upon the native capacities of the soil. But after a few generations of the forests being cleared and the prairies broken, fertility was diminishing, and sustained farming was looking bleak. America, King believed, needed to look East for instruction on how to grow food for the long term.

Among the important insights King learned in his travels was a different perspective on "waste." The Asian farmers treated manure of all kinds as something of great value, if not holy then something very close. "One of the most remarkable agricultural practices adopted by any civilized people is the centuries-long and well nigh universal conservation and utilization of all human waste in China, Korea and Japan, turning it to marvelous account in the maintenance of soil fertility and in the production of food," wrote King.[2]

In Asia, King observed farmers carrying buckets of manure into their fields, mixing it with water and applying it to the soil. It was believed with good reason that manure applied in the right ways to the soil would be incorporated by bacteria that would otherwise neutralize any pathogens. At the time King visited Asia, not only was most human waste utilized in agriculture, but he also observed very few flies. The ecosystem, grounded in the good soil biology of those fields, was quickly incorporating the manure into the earth.

Manure was so central to agriculture that to defecate as a guest at a friend's house was considered leaving a gift. Many farmers would rush out to gather any manure dropped by a passing water buffalo. This was a culture, now mostly lost even in Asia, that saw shit as sacred, a good and valuable tie between our lives and the life of the earth.

Such an understanding is in critical contrast to what King saw as the Western understanding of soil, one that he compared to the use of coal—a resource mined rather than renewed. "Man is the most extravagant accelerator of waste the world has ever endured," he wrote (presumably meaning

---

2. King, *Farmers*, 76.

Western industrial "man").[3] King sounds like a dower prophet here, and indeed the soil depletion that was widespread in 1909 as King wrote these words would lead to the Dust Bowl in the thirties. We still have not learned the lesson of that time—we are repeating the same errors in new guises.

The question we must ask ourselves is why, given manure's life-giving qualities, we turn away from it with disgust? Why does our waste not return to the earth, gathered for compost from which we can grow new life? Why is it not considered a sacred connection, cycling back the force of life to return? Who would want to flush such holy shit down a common sewer?

---

3. King, *Farmers*, 77.

Borders of the Holy

There was a man who lived on the outside. Inside was his family, the networks of relationship in which he had grown up. There was the larger society, made of its festivals, the circles of life—gifts and obligations. And at the center of it all was the temple with its priests. Those inside could worship in the temple, join in the ancient processions with their psalms, witness the grand spaces drawing eyes up to whatever lay beyond. Those on the inside could meet the obligations that were the only way to be in right relationship with God; to offer the correct kind of worship in the temple.

But on the outside, there was no getting in. Inside was called clean, outside unclean. There were many ways to be outside. Usually it was a temporary reality, the time of a woman's period, or coming into contact with a corpse (not as uncommon a thing then as now). But for others it had become their condition—the woman forced into prostitution, the man who decided to betray his kin for a bit of Roman wealth, those with certain diseases of skin or blood that would never clear up. For this man, it was leprosy, a general term for an infectious disease of the skin—it could have been as mild as a chronic rash or as severe as Hansen's disease. Whatever it was, he wanted to be reconnected and returned to the life of the whole.

The priests tried their best, for a fee. But no cure could be found for the man and so the priests had to maintain the borders of exclusion. He would remain outside, doomed to stay there, it seemed. But then there was a man from Galilee, proclaiming something new. He was not a priest, nor even from a priestly class. There was nothing about him that would allow him to make someone clean by the standards of the temple. Instead, this man could make whole, he could heal. He could do the thing the priests could not, for all the fees they collected. And being made whole would mean becoming clean in a way more meaningful than any ritual.

So the man on the outside came to this healer from Galilee. "If you want, you can make me clean," he said. Those words were a trigger. The healer became angry, "incensed." Not at the man on the outside, but at those who kept him there, who preserved the boundary of clean and unclean without seeking to make whole. The healer then did the thing that any person of his culture would refuse to do. He touched the man—an act that could have led to his own uncleanness, not to mention possible infection. With that touch the man said, "I do want to. Be clean!" This cleanness came not by the certification of any priest, but through one life being restored to wholeness. It was then, when the man was made whole and clean, that the healer Jesus told the man to go to the priests and show himself to them. Not to ask for their certification, signing off on his cleanness, but as a "testimony against them."

This scene from the first chapter of Mark's Gospel is a pattern we see repeated, over and over in the life of Jesus and throughout the Gospels. He is one who has come to make whole and to confuse the borders of the holy, the clean and the unclean. In doing this, Jesus created a new path for being human—a way that goes beyond our fear of death that is at the heart of so many of our borders and boundaries.

It is fear of death that so easily turns to disgust and thus a partitioning of life. In Ernest Becker's *The Denial of Death,* he argues that our disgust at shit is rooted in our aversion to death. For Becker the human creature finds itself split between animality (represented by death, decay, and shit) and spirit, the symbolic mind. As he puts it: "Man is literally split in two: he has an awareness of his own splendid uniqueness in that he sticks out of nature with a towering majesty, and yet he goes back into the ground a few feet in order blindly and dumbly to rot and disappear forever."[1]

This split at the core of the human self comes to the fore in what the psychoanalytic tradition has called the problem of anality—the attempt of someone to "protect himself against the accidents of life and danger of death . . . trying to pass himself off as anything but an animal." When we call someone "anal" or "anal-retentive" we still, far from having a grasp of the psychoanalytic origins of those terms, mean someone who is forcibly in control, someone who cannot tolerate change, chance, or mess. The anal

---

1. Becker, *Denial of Death,* 259.

person is the one who tries to hold "it" in and therefore denies the reality of their own shit.

"The upsetting thing about anality," writes Becker, "is that it reveals that all culture, all man's creative life-ways, are in some basic part of them a fabricated protest against natural reality, a denial of the truth of the human condition, and an attempt to forget the pathetic creature that man is."[2] What Jesus does, taking on the life of the "pathetic creature," is to break the border between the heights and the valleys, the sky and the dirt. Heaven has come here, it is at hand, Jesus taught. In him we find not a liberation from the shit of the earth, but a path of humility through which we discover that shit is holy and so are we, all connected in the great circle of creation's wholeness.

---

2. Becker, *Denial*, 172.

Scum of the Earth

There's a hassle in dealing with compost. It requires work, tending, a collection of the right materials. It is so unlike the "trash" picked up in neat bins by machines with robot arms. At the very moment I write, I can hear the trash truck moving along my street. It comes every week, hauling away the bags we've placed in the large plastic bin by the curb. The whole process is only slightly more trouble than a toilet's flush. I've never been to the city dump here, but I have seen them in other places, so I can imagine what it all looks like—a mountain of plastic bags, a bulldozer pushing them into pits to be buried, pipes eventually pushed down into the hill to let out the methane from decay. But like I said, I've never been and that is part of the problem.

The late literary critic Harold Bloom said that Gnosticism is the American religion, and there is no better evidence for how right he is than how we treat our trash. Our desire for the pure life, the clean, a way of being free from the troubles of biological existence (death and refuse, decay and excrement) is at its base an attempt to escape the materiality of our lives as creatures. To be a biological being is to be inescapably tied to the metabolisms of the earth which means death and life, eating and excrement.

Gnostic comes from the Greek word for knowledge. It is most literally the one who knows. It doesn't take much imagination to see a link between this idea of knowing and the story of Adam and Eve in the garden of Eden, seeking to transcend their creatureliness with knowledge. But the Gnosticism that develops later sees knowledge, usually of a secretive and esoteric type, as the basis of power and the ability to rise to new planes of spiritual existence.

In the Greco-Roman world of the second century, gnostic spiritualists often adopted and appropriated Christian teachings. Though their cults faded, the gnostic impulse has continued in varied forms including "New Age" spiritualisms, some of which have taken up the gnostic name again.

Though these broad groups varied in specifics, most gnostics believed that the physical world—the world of flesh, of death with its rotting bodies and shit, its stench of decay, were the source of evil. Their aim was liberation from the physical, a liberation that would carry one into the pure realm of spirit where true wisdom was the ultimate expression of the divine. The gnostics, in some of their hierarchies, placed the Jewish God toward the middle—a god, but a lesser one on account of his fondness for mud and blood. If Jesus was on the hierarchy, it was often a Docetic version—a Jesus who only appeared to be embodied but was in fact purely spiritual, thus disconnected from physical life.

The gnostics wanted to save God and save the human spirit from the creation, the "unacceptable" reality of the material world. They saw shit as a flaw and so they denied it, entering a long tradition of rejection not only of our excrement but our entanglements with the world. Excrement is what keeps us from being gods unbound from earth. Shit is the sign that we are moments in a continuum of life rather than spiritual beings standing outside it. If you want to transcend creaturely existence, as many gnostics did, then it's best to keep your distance from manure.

Milan Kundera's narrator in the novel *The Unbearable Lightness of Being* brilliantly expresses the gnostic view:

> The fact that until recently the word "shit" appeared in print as s— has nothing to do with moral considerations. You can't claim that shit is immoral, after all! The objection to shit is a metaphysical one. The daily defecation session is daily proof of the unacceptability of Creation. Either/Or: either shit is acceptable (in which case don't lock yourself in the bathroom!) or we are created in an unacceptable manner.[1]

Kundera's narrator says that European faiths—from Christianity to Communism—live in the embrace of Genesis 1 with its celebration of the goodness of creation and godlike role for humans. But for Kundera the shadow side of creation, excrement and death and decay, are counter to this vision of light and goodness. And so rather than readjusting our vision, letting the story of Genesis 2 in which humans are made of earth guide us, we deny the earth and all that attaches us to it—death and manure.

---

1. Kundera, *Unbearable Lightness of Being*, 248.

Scum of the Earth

St. Paul was anything but a gnostic. His vision of faith in Christ was rooted in the depths of Jewish hope and understanding, an affirmation of the world of people and animals, rocks and trees. And Paul, like Jesus before him, sought to dissolve the borders of clean and unclean. In his first letter to the Corinthians, Paul says that the apostles, those bringing the message of Christ into the world, were like the "scum of the earth." They were the refuse, literally the "thing cleansed away."

Paul is using this as a metaphor with his typical rhetorical flair, but in his description he is naming a reality of the humble life. In humility we move away from the godlike ambitions of power, of an unearthly purity, and back toward the thrown-off things that reconnect us to the flows of life. Just as Jesus moved in humility toward the earth, taking on a body of human flesh, a body that must eat of the earth and return its excrement to it, so we are invited to be reconnected to the truly human life. The world is made holy not through transcendence but recognition—all things are clean in their wholeness, holy in their life as creatures.

In the incarnation, this descent and ascent, creation was changed because Jesus joined with the scum of the earth, turning it from the refuse of a system that sought liberation from humanity and into a source of compost and new life. And in doing this, Jesus helped to reconnect the severed ties of human life, the essential bonds we share with all creation. None of us are alone; we are all a network of living things.

To be human is to be a kind of landscape—a living site where an abundance of other creatures make their homes, deep in the interior of the land or along and around its edges. Our guts are a raucous gathering of bacteria, our lungs a forest of fungi, our skin an interchange as busy as O'Hare airport just before Christmas. As the mycologist Merlin Sheldrake suggests, rather than saying how are you doing, we should say how are y'all doing.

But it is not only our cells that play host to other forms of life. The very energy I am using to write these words may reflect a symbiosis, one that has become so established and static that it is impossible to name where one organism ends and the other begins. This idea was pioneered by the scientist Lynn Margulis who argued that the very energy core of our bodies found in mitochondria, the organelles in our cells that create the basic form of energy our body uses in the form of Adinosene TriPhosphate (ATP), are, in fact, an ancient microbe that formed a close symbiosis with another creature. They became so tightly linked that they in some way fused together and continued to evolve into the varied Eukaryotic life we now see.[2]

To be human is then to be an entangled site of many creatures, each contributing to the health and existence of the whole. And if Jesus is God incarnate, God become *human*, then Christ too must be entangled with the creation in this way. The human and divine Christ must have had E. coli in his gut and aspergillus fungi in his lungs. Christ ate food and lived as the home of bacteria and fungi. Like most people of his time and place he likely hosted parasitic nematodes in his gut. Christ gave a shit for the sake of the world in all the flourishing senses of that phrase.

If God entered the world and became a part of its continuum, then perhaps the world is now infused with the divine. What if the bacteria now living in my gut are related to the bacteria that once lived in the intestines of Christ? What if Christ has now infected the world with the divine—slowly spreading, slowly fusing, and thus creating something new? What if the entangled body of Jesus has entangled all things in the God-human Christ?

2. Montgomery, *Hidden Half,* 52–58.

The Grail of the World

My first experiences of place were in the woods of my childhood. My family lived at that time in East Texas, a rural cabin surrounded by a small patch of forest. Through the forest was a lake and beyond it horse pastures. All were in the territory of my play and exploration. Beneath a towering pine, I would find owl pellets filled with small bones, the tiny skeletons of mice. In a muddy creek bed I once encountered an alligator snapping turtle the size of a side table, its head as large as a softball. And here and there in the woods, I would find evidence of the Caddo tribe that had lived here before the white settlers came—a paint stone, rubbed smooth by thumbs crushing berries, the shards of knapping stone tools. To step beyond the doors of the house was to enter a realm of possibility, a place that was alive with wonder.

When I saw my first Indiana Jones movie, *Indiana Jones and the Last Crusade*,[1] I found a narrative that captured the sense of adventure I felt when I entered the woods. I soon acquired a felt fedora and a braided leather whip. Hat on and whip coiled at my side, I walked through the pine forests and fields as though I were Indy traipsing through an Egyptian desert. Indiana Jones gave me a story in which I could see the story of my own discoveries. Here too there were hidden treasures; here too there were obstacles to their discovery to be overcome.

I have seen the same adventuring spirit in my daughters. My oldest, for her six-year-old birthday, planned a party around digging for artifacts. She asked for her own geologist hammer and trowel, and with those gifts in hand, she led a crew of children to a small, excavated pit by an old school down the street. Ahead of time I scattered a few "treasures" in the pit, but the children armed with shovels and trowels found plenty of their own. From quartz crystals to bottle caps—they were occupied for hours and wouldn't

---

1. Hollywood: Paramount, 1989.

have quit for any lure less than cake. Their imaginations were open to the wonder of the place, and they knew that any rusted piece of metal, any misshapen rock, could be part of a story of those who once shared this ground, whether prehistoric mollusks or the children who attended the school a century ago.

The legend of the grail shares in this work of imagination. The most famous grail legends are those rooted in the Arthurian tradition. They are stories of Joseph of Arimathea carrying the cup of Christ to the English shore. In the tradition, the grail is not only the cup that Jesus used at the Last Supper, but also the cup with which Joseph caught the blood and water that spilled from the side of Christ when his side was pierced by a Roman soldier's spear.

Like so many medieval relic stories, the Arthurian grail legends are about a grand narrative coming near. What could seem like an abstract story about people in a faraway place becomes concrete and close. This critical object of the story, the very cup of Christ, could be beneath the ground of any English field.

I walk across my garden, it is late August, the grass is brittle. Yesterday I went in search of migrating shorebirds near the river. A field that had been flooded most of the summer is nearly dry, a few puddles here and there, hundreds of dead carp lined its shores. There were a few migrating sandpipers huddled around the puddles, but mostly there were vultures and crows scavenging among the fish.

August is the hardest month here. The growth of June and July with their summer storms has given way to clear skies and merciless heat. Most gardeners give up tending their patches as the heat passes 100 each day. This is when we pray for rain, but then reconsider for it often comes with flooding.

I find it hard to have much imagination for my yard this time of year. It is a month where air conditioning, the compromise I wish I could live without, is a welcome respite—its fan a lulling force. And yet, what if I could imagine the grail of Christ here? What if this ground, broken as it is, contained some trace of Christ's body. Could I find a relic of the Risen One so close at hand?

It is possible. Sergei Bulgakov, an Orthodox theologian of the early twentieth century, wrote in his essay, "The Holy Grail," that when Christ's side was pierced: "The blood and water that flowed into the world abide in the world." For Bulgakov, the legend of the grail enables us to imagine a way in which Christ continues to abide on earth, even though Christ has also ascended into heaven. "The image of the Holy Grail, in which the holy blood of Christ is kept, expresses precisely the idea that, even though the Lord ascended in His honorable flesh to heaven, the world received His holy relic in the blood and water that flowed out of His side." Then comes his shocking conclusion: "And the whole world is the chalice of the Holy Grail."[2]

Bulgakov spends a good deal of the early part of his essay exploring the ways that blood has traditionally been a mediating substance between body and spirit. For blood to pour from Christ into the earth means that an aspect of both Christ's human life and his divine presence remain in the creation. The world is entangled with Christ and through such an entanglement it is transformed.

When I stand in my yard, then, I am standing upon the grail. I don't need to make a pilgrimage or quest. My work is one of seeing, of recognizing the sacred cup upon which I stand. A journey that leads to visions is, of course, how so many of the best quests work. They are stories of learning to see what was already there, or being prepared to see what one will encounter.

But what if the world is also more than the grail, the vessel that received Christ's presence? What if the entanglement of Christ and the cosmos began even before the blood poured from Jesus's side into the ready ground that caught it?

That Christ became human, entering the particular realities of a place, must mean that Christ's entanglement began as soon as God became a creature. We can add to the legend of the grail with the story of ecology—the way in which no human person is alone, all of us are a multitude of interrelationships in our bodies and beyond our bodies.

Before Christ spilled blood into the earth he ate food grown from soil and he defecated back a microbe-rich return of nutrients to the soil. Before water poured into Joseph's cup at the cross, Jesus pissed a nitrogen-rich stream, somewhere along the road from Nazareth, perhaps watering a mustard plant. The point is that Christ's offering of life for the world started long before the cross and was far more literal than the metaphors of bread. "This is my body" becomes "these are my bodies"—a continual offering.

2. Bulgakov, *Holy Grail*, 33.

To see shit, not as the embarrassing evidence of our animality but as a reminder of our life within the whole of creation, is to learn to move beyond the conflict between body and soul, spirit and flesh. God became human so that humanity might become gods, said St. Athanasius in his great book on the Incarnation. But what if it is more than that? What if the truth is that God became human so that humans could become creatures once more, reminded by Jesus of what it means to be connected to the flows of life? What if to be fully human is to move again into a life that rests in the divine?

Such a reality would fit a humble God, a God who is not interested in subservient creatures, bowing before the divine. This is the God who becomes an obedient creature, a servant, in order to show us the way to be fully human, the lost art of being a creature.

Return

The path to the promised land is all around us; all that's required is to humbly follow rather than hold on to the vanity that requires a road of our own making.

DANIEL MAYS, *THE NO-TILL ORGANIC VEGETABLE FARM*

As God bends low to love us where we are, we must be open to welcome God in our lives, to embrace this God of humble love and allow God to live in us in every way. Every breath of life must be the breath of God. This is divination. The humility of God's love in some way demands a human response because it is hidden and unobtrusive and quietly sustains life without force or manipulation. It is the role of Christians to publicly witness to the humility of God's faithful love, and this is nothing short of making Christ live anew.

ILIA DELIO, *THE HUMILITY OF GOD*

Sent Your Son

We are gathered in a semicircle, some sitting on camp chairs hauled in slings, others on picnic blankets spread across the leaves. There are fallen logs here and there, additional seating for those who came only with their bodies. In the distance we can hear the metallic "pink" of an aluminum bat and the cheers of a small crowd at the baseball diamond below, but louder and closer are the calls of red-breasted nuthatches newly arrived from the boreal forests and the cries of blue jays patrolling the woods for invading hawks and owls. Not far from where we are gathered a gray squirrel digs into the leaf litter, storing an acorn or planting an oak, depending on the necessities of the winter and the prowess of her memory.

I stand before a pile of stones—small boulders of quartz and sandstone. On top a large piece of shale, hauled up from the creek bed below, makes a table. On it is a clay chalice and patten, the cup filled with wine the plate with bread, home baked just hours before. Around the dishes are flowers and pinecones, nuts and mushrooms—placed there by those gathered as a token of their reflections upon the Gospel. This is a service of church in the woods—liturgy taken beyond the walls and into the creation, Eucharist offered on an altar of unhewn stone.

I bow and all those around bow, as we say:

Holy, Holy, Holy Lord, God of power and might,
heaven and earth are full of your glory.
    Hosanna in the highest.
Blessed is he who comes in the name of the Lord.
    Hosanna in the highest.

A chickadee calls from the trees above. I look around at those gathered. They are framed by the gold of the hickory leaves, beginning the march of fall colors, their bon voyage, the good journey before the empty space of winter. Soon the oaks will follow and the cherries and elms. The trails of this park will take on a new sound, the swish and crunch of brittle carpet. For now, though, it is last year's leaves that cover the forest floor, held in place by the spindled webs of mycelium running white between the fresh food at the surface and the chocolate humus beneath.

As I read aloud the prayers, my hands are lifted in the "orans position" of public prayer, gesturing upwards. This is the embodied sign that though I am the only one speaking, this is not my prayer but ours, all of us gathered here:

> *Holy and gracious Father: In your infinite love you made us for yourself, and, when we had fallen into sin and become subject to evil and death, you, in your mercy, sent Jesus Christ, your only and eternal Son, to share our human nature, to live and die as one of us, to reconcile us to you, the God and Father of all.*
>
> *He stretched out his arms upon the cross, and offered himself, in obedience to your will, a perfect sacrifice for the whole world.*

These lines are rooted in two millennia of prayers—Eastern, Catholic, and Reformed—shaped by each like water and wind upon a rock, breaking it down into the local soil of their varied traditions. The version of the prayer I'm offering on this day is the most Anglican of our eucharistic liturgies, the one named "Prayer A," in *The Book of Common Prayer*. This liturgy is the one most similar to that penned by Thomas Cranmer at the beginning of the English Reformation. It is a beautiful prayer and a practical one, the default of my tradition. Theologically, however, I prefer the longer "Prayer D." This liturgy is the most ecumenical and ancient of our eucharistic rites—originating in West Syria and sharing its modern form in the Anglican, Eastern Orthodox, and Roman Catholic communions. It offers this version of the history of our salvation, the language flowery but the theology fuller:

> *We acclaim you, holy Lord, glorious in power. Your mighty works reveal your wisdom and love. You formed us in your own image, giving the whole world into our care, so that, in obedience to you, our Creator, we might rule and serve all your creatures. When our disobedience took us far from you, you did not abandon us to the power of death. In your mercy you came to our help, so that in seeking you we might find you. Again and again you called us into covenant with you, and through the prophets you taught us to hope for salvation.*
>
> *Father, you loved the world so much that in the fullness of time you sent your only Son to be our Savior. Incarnate by the Holy Spirit,*

> born of the Virgin Mary, he lived as one of us, yet without sin. To the poor he proclaimed the good news of salvation; to prisoners, freedom; to the sorrowful, joy. To fulfill your purpose he gave himself up to death; and, rising from the grave, destroyed death, and made the whole creation new.
> And, that we might live no longer for ourselves, but for him who died and rose for us, he sent the Holy Spirit, his own first gift for those who believe, to complete his work in the world, and to bring to fulfillment the sanctification of all.

It's a longer prayer, used by most churches for the big holidays of the Christian year—All Saints', Easter, the Feast of the Ascension. In both prayers the story of salvation is offered. It is a story that centers on a return, a reconciliation by which we join again in the circle of God's family. The D prayer shows, better than A, that this is something that is true not only for humankind but for the whole of creation. Jesus came, died and rose, not only to reconcile humanity to God, but also to make "the whole creation new."

For that renewal to happen, the prayers speak of a descent, a going down like the fall of leaves that rot into humus to renew the ground. Christ accomplished that same pattern of descent and renewal on a cosmic scale, once and for the whole of the creation.

Death is apocalyptic—it reveals, it opens up. In death many finally come to the truth of themselves, confess the lies they've harbored over lifetimes. It can be that, but not everyone who dies lets go, not everyone discovers the catharsis of the self death can make possible. I have a colleague who worked in a hospital as part of her training to be a priest. She witnessed a family yelling and screaming and fighting around the death bed of an old man. The man joined in the uproar, disparaging his daughters, unwilling to end with reconciliation. "People die how they live," an old nurse told the chaplain as she stood in shock outside the room. But that is not the only possibility. In death we have a chance to come to the truth about ourselves and the world. We have to surrender to the loss of self, however. "Those who seek their lives will lose them, but those who lose their lives for my sake will find them."

The prayer moves on to the "words of institution"—this is my body, this is my blood, do this in remembrance of me. While a version of these words are found in Matthew, Mark, and Luke (as well as First Corinthians), the Gospel of John lacks them. Instead, John's version of the Last Supper tells the story of Jesus washing the feet of the disciples. Much has been written on this difference of the Fourth Gospel, but I think it is possible to see in it a eucharistic act beyond bread and wine—an act of offering, a command to become the servants of all that is, a way of being that is at the heart of the eucharistic life of the church.

In the Eucharist prayer, after offering the bread and the wine to his disciples, Jesus concludes by saying that whenever you do this "do it in remembrance of me." I can't shake the possibilities of the English here—to re-member—to literally bring the body back together. The Greek word is *anamnesis*—an active recollection, a bringing to mind. Jesus of course said these words in neither Greek nor English. He spoke Aramaic, most likely. I wonder at the meaning in that language, but the English does good work theologically, for what is resurrection but a remembering? Is not the hope of resurrection the hope that God will remember us, not simply by calling us to mind, but by re-membering our bodies and souls, our connections and community in a new creation?

> *Christ has died*
> *Christ has risen*
> *Christ will come again*

Death is not the end—that's the Christian story, but it is also the story of creation. Life is constantly rising, teeming, generating from what has "died." It is annihilation that we must fear—when death has parted with renewal, when bodies can no longer hope for resurrection. This is the reality we call sin—a captivity in which our selves are disconnected from the source of their life in God and creation.

St. Paul talked about this condition as a kind of enslavement. This wasn't an abstract metaphor for him. Many in the audience would have been enslaved persons—those who daily suffered the rape, exploitation, beatings, and abuse that were common for many in a first-century Roman household. Paul wrote that with Christ people could find freedom, but that freedom had to come through death and death was the only way out for many slaves.

Freedom through death was a reality in American chattel slavery as well. When escaping alive wasn't possible, many enslaved people chose suicide as the path of liberation. This, of course, was not in the economic interests of the slaveholders. In the Haitian plantations of the Caribbean, through a collusion between vodou priests and the slaveholders, there developed a belief that suicide would prevent one from moving on to the afterlife. This is where we get the idea of the zombie.

Using traditional African religion, and beliefs that had developed in the Haitian colonies, enslaved people were taught that those who committed suicide would not be granted safe passage back to "heavenly Africa." They would be neither dead, nor alive. They would become the living dead and these living dead would be slaves forever. No heaven, no resurrection— a zombie in the traditional sense is not like the dead returned to life but rather one who has lost one's life but never been allowed to die. There is no possibility of reunion and remembrance.

We have become a people for whom the zombie is a familiar figure, a symbolic possibility. We dread death and so we seek to stop it. We are afraid to let our bodies, our culture, our institutions fade, and so we keep them from dying. In doing so we stop the flow that allows death to turn toward decay, that unravels the elements of our being so that new life can be formed. The result is not life eternal but the living dead, moving mindlessly through the world, giving nothing, consuming everything. It is a terrifying annihilation of the human person and with it the creation with which we are entangled.

In answer to this we have the death of Jesus, God dying so that we might live. In letting go of his life Jesus was simply enacting what he had long taught his disciples, a truth we can find in the ecological realities of any place—to live we must die. It is in this willingness to let go of life that Jesus is able to enact new life in the world at its deepest level—the healing of creation, its renewal from the depths.

After the Lord's prayer is said, I break the bread and then move around the circle, placing a piece in each outstretched hand—"The Body of Christ, the Bread of Heaven." I follow with the cup—"The Blood of Christ, the Cup of Salvation." There is always wine left over, and so finally it is poured on the ground as an offering. The earth again becomes the grail.

As the people move back to their seats, their feet stir the leaves. I smell the scent of soil in the air, the smell of microbes in their trillions beneath me. Somewhere overhead I can make out the sound of geese, traveling south along their ancient routes. For a moment I can feel the life of this place, a life caught up in the life of Christ, who lives even now in the fullness of the cosmos. Christ is the heart of creation, the ancient writers claimed. Christ who became human, who took the form of a common peasant, is at the heart of the whole vast world. This is a mystery at the heart of being—the mystery of God coming among us, of God becoming small so that we may become human. It is the mystery of kenosis and incarnation, emptiness and flesh. It is this that makes every mass a Christ-mass.

Blue Christmas

Christmas trees have always been a point of conflict in my family, mostly because of my curmudgeonly resistance. Plastic and silk? Of course not. A potted cedar? Most are non-native, potentially invasive. A cut tree? Hauled miles with the use of fossil fuels from what is likely the tree version of a feedlot.

The best year was when my family went with my plan of purchasing a potted Yaupon holly. It's a native tree species, evergreen, and it came pre-decorated with lovely red berries. My daughters named it "Holly" and she still lives in our yard, growing and happy, providing food for the mockingbirds and White-throated Sparrows and evergreen cover throughout the year.

In subsequent years, however, we searched nurseries in vain for an American holly tree or other native plant alternative. Giving up on my dissent, my wife declared that we would purchase cut trees from the local School for the Blind, helping fund a good cause that is mere blocks from our house. Out voted, I've mostly gone along with the plan.

In the fall of 2020, after months of political turmoil and pandemic disease, it came time to get a Christmas tree once again. Shortly after Thanksgiving we passed by the tree lot at the school and noticed that, though they'd only started selling trees, hardly any were left. "We need to go get a tree soon!" my wife exclaimed. "I'm sure they'll get more in," I answered, still dragging my feet. Thankfully, Emily went with our daughters one dreary day and picked a tree. It was one of the last ones available and no more were coming. The man selling her the tree said that it was the fastest they'd ever sold out. A trend that was noted around the country. It seems that people, mostly stuck at home with precious little cheer in their lives wanted to get this representation of continued life and the memories of better times as soon as possible.

What happened with trees has been happening in other ways with Christmas for a long while in the United States. The season that once began with Advent or, according to a more secular calendar, just after Thanksgiving, has been steadily moving earlier into the year. It is not uncommon now to see Christmas advertised in October.

I once heard an excellent sermon reflecting on this fact. The preacher suggested that our extension of Christmas is a way for us to sing with joy over the dark realities of our world. Instead of facing them, entering their pain, we just raise our voices louder with our desperate cheer, hoping to overwhelm the sadness with our songs.

I think this suggestion is right, for the most part, and among its worst tragedies is how out of step it is with Christmas itself. All the warm glow, the happy songs, the feasting and celebration and community that we are told to feel at Christmas ignores the central fact at the holiday's center—God came among us to enter our limits, share in our suffering, die like any mortal. Christmas is about joy amid sorrow, not an undoing of it.

The English monastic John Chapman articulated the tragic reality of Christmas in a letter to the Mother of a convent:

> May we learn to become very little with our Lord, if He is to do great things in us, as we wish . . . It is a cruel road that He has chosen, taking our miseries and our sufferings, in order to be able to give us His joy and His glory. He makes our road very easy in comparison, though we complain, and think He is very cruel to us. I always feel the Crib so sad, as well as so sweet. It is not like Easter, which is nothing but rejoicing.[1]

What Chapman sees is the heart of the Incarnation, which is a glorious gift to humanity, but also a sad and tragic reality for God. Christ entered a world of suffering, in deep solidarity with all those who live not with joy but with pain. If we love Christ, we must also mourn the trauma of Christ's scars, recognizing in them the scars that will come inevitably to all who follow him. To "become very little with our Lord," as Chapman writes, is to join in the solidarity of Christ, a solidarity with the very lowly.

It is no wonder that it is from the Franciscans that we have some of our greatest Christmas traditions. The images of the nativity, as now conceived, were born of the Franciscan imagination. And yet it was Francis who understood that to be close to Christ we must live in solidarity with

---

1. Chapman, *Spiritual Letters*, 117.

the lowly, a lowliness we could find especially in the Eucharist. As Francis wrote to his order:

> The Lord of the universe,
> God and the Son of God,
> so humbles Himself
> that for our salvation
> He hides Himself
> under an ordinary piece of bread!
> Brothers, look at the humility of God,
> and *pour out your hearts before Him!*
> Humble yourselves
> that you may be exalted by Him!
> Hold nothing back to yourselves for yourselves
> that He Who gives Himself totally to you
> may receive you totally.[2]

Though suffering is involved, this lowly path is also a way into joy. Francis found joy in being with the outcasts of society, being with the wild creatures who lived beyond the usefulness of the mercantile economy. He counted himself as a troubadour for Christ, one who sang in celebration of his love for God, a fool who was overwhelmed by his desire for the beloved. But like any true love, Francis knew that devotion requires a limiting of ourselves—a focusing and subjugation of our dreams, our egos, the expansive play of our powers. Christ became low for the sake of love and so became limited, but it was through those limits that he proved, paradoxically, the fullness of his power.

It is ironic that Christ's entering into limits, the Incarnation that is marked by Christ's descent, would be celebrated as Christmas now is in the Western world. Our boundless and unfettered yes to all of our desires, our spending in excess, our accumulation of debts and the more of our material lives is how we have come to celebrate the great self-emptying act of Christ who came among us in love.

In the United States there has been a recent effort to put the "Christ into Christmas," an amorphous rebellion against the culture at large turning Christmas into the more generic "holidays." Such efforts are mostly confused, mixing commerce, patriotism, and faith into a uniquely American mess. But perhaps we should be like a good improv actor, saying "yes" and raising them one. What if we renew Christmas as a celebration of the

---

2. Quoted in Delio, *Humility of God*, 29–30.

Incarnation; a time when Christians resist the madness of our commerce and recognize instead the gifts already among us? What if Christmas is a time when we become little, living with less on less? What if Christmas is a time when we offer our skill rather than our savings accounts (or more likely our credit cards), hospitality rather than hoarding? Limiting and offering—that is the true spirit of Christmas for it is the spirit of the Incarnation.

Such a celebration would honor the wonder as well as the tragedy of the coming of Christ in the manger—the pain of Mary in birth as prelude to the pain of Mary's loss at the cross, the joy of the shepherds at the Good News as an icon of the empty tomb of Easter. The Incarnation is a reality of joy and grief, as is any human life lived in fullness. So it is that Christmas is among the most human of our feasts, a humanity that can be claimed only if we see the hint of creation's shadow at the same time that we stand in the radiance of God's good light—Christ's becoming poor as we become poor in response and thereby find our fullness.

Kenotic Ecology

My first class in permaculture was in the living room of Casa de Anna Schultz, the home and teaching center of Ched Myers and Elaine Enns. I was in California for the Bartimaeus Institute, convened by Myers and Enns, where lectures on Scripture and theology were set alongside plays and dances, with workshops exploring everything from herbalism to community car repair.

The workshop I attended on permaculture was taught by Chris Grataski, a farmer and permaculture designer from Virginia. Chris is one of those rare people who has read widely and remembers most of what he reads, bringing into his teaching everything from management theory to post-structuralist theology to soil science, blended in a seamless way. In this short overview of permaculture, that synthesis was at play—an abundance easily spilling over the allotted time to no one's complaints.

Chris began with the key concepts of permaculture, the sort one might find in any course—permaculture ethics and design principles, the basic outline of zones and the "permaculture flower." But woven within those were Chris's reflections on the theology of permaculture. For Chris, permaculture wasn't simply a way of thinking about ecological landscape design; permaculture was a way of living out the Christian call to kenosis.

Kenosis, the self-emptying way of Christ, is a concept that would seem at the heart of all the reasons Nietzsche found Christianity distasteful—a limiting of brilliance and power in order to make room for the downtrodden, the "scum of the earth" (1 Cor 4:13). Kenosis hardly seems like a concept that would lead to the affirmation of life, the cultivation of flourishing. And yet, rightly understood it is just that, for it is an emptying not for the sake of diminishment, but of abundance. Like the clearing of a monocultural field for a dynamic and multilayered food forest. Kenosis is the opening necessary for new life to begin and be joined by an ever expanding fractal of emergence.

A good and functioning ecosystem is not one of competing individuals, all in a war for limited resources. Rather it is a multitude supported by mutuality, exchange, and support. This is what God gathers in the church at its best, not a subsuming of many people and cultures into an abstract unity, but a joining and linking into a common and varied life all those rooted in the earth. For such life to happen it must make room, it must be kenotic, and to do so it must move toward the humus, it must be humble.

Some years after my first class with Chris, I invited him to come to the church I was serving to lead a full 72-hour Permaculture Design Course. There, gathered in an old classroom with a wild mix of grandmothers, herbalists, circus clowns, and pipeline blockaders, we absorbed as much as we could of the rushing river of Chris's knowledge. There he explained to us that one way to understand permaculture is as "applied disturbance ecology" or "planned succession."

All ecosystems go through cycles of growth and succession. A prairie burns making room for new growth, a tree dies making room in the canopy. Old makes way for new and grows old again, and at each stage there are niches, levels of abundance. But succession does not always work to create the nourishing abundance of life. Ecosystems can get off balance, the disturbance can become more trauma than hospitality. Human abuse of the land has offset the patterns of succession. Instead of oaks and native pines maturing into a stable forest we get nandina and privet, introduced species that take over and leave little room for the evolved diversity of native forests.

Permaculture works with the process of succession and seeks to guide it in a pattern that bends toward the health of the whole, providing for human flourishing at the same time as the health of the ecosystem. A conventional farmer might brag of yield per acre of a crop, but such a harvest likely comes at the expense of other creatures. When I heard the permaculturalist Mark Shepherd speak about his farm, he talked of the way his turnip crop helped build his soil and the variety of bird species nesting on his land. His aims were for more than a single measure of success—he was cultivating and shaping the land, but he was doing so in a kenotic form—a way that makes room.

Kenotic Ecology

One afternoon, during the design course, we went to a local Audubon sanctuary, much of it being actively reclaimed after abuse. At its edge was a more mature forest bordering a glade. It was there that Chris had us spread out, each of us finding a sit spot where we could simply be still to watch and listen, smell and feel. It was a kind of contemplative exercise—one in which we were invited to welcome, for a moment, the fullness of life around us. The smell of the rotting leaves; the movement of a carpenter ant at the base of a tree; the mushroom, white toped and gilled, fruiting from the side of a fallen log; the sound of a thrasher, searching for food among the leaf litter. We sat, taking it all in.

Chris's point in this exercise was to teach us one of the critical realities of any kenotic agriculture. We begin, not by acting, but by stopping. We draw back and listen. We learn to wait and see what emerges. We try, as best we can, to understand what we are disturbing before we do anything. It is only after we have embraced the blessed poverty of that emptying that we can begin the work of cultivation.

To move forward after this watching and observing, however, is not to act because we now know. We have not somehow comprehended the landscape and are now able to act within it confidently. Instead, our waiting and watching has allowed us to enter the mystery of the place. It is in working in such mystery that we act in a truly human way.

Kenosis is not the reach of power into poverty, providing solutions for what experts know is the problem. It is a giving up of power, of the heights, in order to enter the mystery of suffering, growth, and life. To act humbly in a landscape, or in a relationship of any kind, is to act in full awareness that we are involved in a mystery that is knowable in connection and yet incomprehensible as a whole.

Thoughts While Pushing a Wheelbarrow

One winter day, when the sun was shining and the cold was invigorating and crisp, I called a local tree company about some mulch. Fine mulch, of the kind sold by landscaping companies, is great for those who can afford it. But the rougher woodchips, ground down by the crews who remove fallen trees or clear powerlines, is usually free for the taking, especially if you can save them the hassle of hauling the chips to a proper dump site. I called and the tree company promised a foreman would bring a load first thing in the morning.

At 7 am, a large truck pulled up full of wood chips, still green from the fresh cut. Mostly these were the remains of branches, cut along roads and powerlines, which was preferable for my purposes. Wood chips from hardwood branches, called ramial chips, are better for developing soil because of the types of polymers and other compounds in these newer growth woods. I would use them to mulch beds, make compost, build paths, and grow mushrooms—woodchips are a miracle medium and largely a free one.

Five men piled out of the cab, all Spanish speakers with one young foreman who was fluently bilingual. My plan had been for them to back the truck down my driveway and dump the chips in my backyard where they would be out of the way. But when I suggested it, the foreman looked doubtful. He and the driver spoke in a flurry of Spanish and then the foreman turned to me, "We think we'll crack your driveway with the weight of the truck." It was that much mulch.

We settled on a plan of dumping the woodchips at the end of my driveway by the street. In the end the pile was nearly five feet high, twenty feet long, and ten feet wide. I spent the next eight hours with a wheelbarrow and a pitch fork—loading and hauling wood chips to varied piles and paths around my yard.

Thoughts While Pushing a Wheelbarrow

A day of manual labor is a gift, and I often like to keep my mind free during such work. But with the length of the day ahead, I decided to mix my time with silence and listening to essays by Wendell Berry, read by the actor Nick Offerman, collected in *The World-Ending Fire*.[1]

I pitched and pushed, hauled and raked. When I finished an essay, I'd put the headphones in my pocket for a while and then pick them up again after several more wheelbarrows full of mulch were taken here and there. As the day moved forward and the warmth grew, neighbors emerged, and my work would be interrupted by welcome conversation. This neighborly conviviality is the best part of urban life. Though I often long to live out, away from the dominance of the manufactured world, it is these moments of human happening that I know I'd miss the most.

James, who lives in a house catty-cornered from mine, wandered over. He's in his late sixties, I'd guess. A black man who once worked as a welder. He and his wife Vernastine often bring over treats and toys for my daughters, and James works with his son to reclaim old bikes, fix them up and give them to kids that have none. He plays guitar on his porch in the warm weather, singing the blues. When complimented he's always self-deprecating—"oh it just sounds like an old cat dying."

On this day, James wandered over to look in the construction dumpster across the street. There's an old school there, now abandoned through consolidation. It was being renovated to apartments and office space, the dumpster daily collecting useful scraps of all kinds. James would go by several times a week to collect the metal scraps being torn from the building—kitchen vent hoods, wiring, duct work. After accumulating a trailer full, James would take it to a scrap metal yard and convert what would otherwise have been trash into a useful bit of extra money.

I have known a number of people like James over the years—practical and resourceful, unwilling to let something of value go to waste. They take what is refuse for the overfed, speeding world that has no time to waste and so makes a waste of the world. It is people like James who have found the possibility of real wealth in the midst of this waste. Wealth in any meaningful and lasting sense is the ability to live well with fewer supports, dependencies only on the fundamentals of life, the things that truly matter.

When I run through the scenarios of possible apocalypse, be it local like a tornado or global like total economic collapse, I am glad that James is my neighbor. He's the kind of person who knows how to do things and

---

1. Recorded Books, 2020.

will know what to do when things fall apart. That to me is worth far more than having the latest iPhone or driving a car that won't be operable when the grid fails.

James is not unusual in my neighborhood, though he's an exemplar of those virtues. My neighborhood is not poor, but neither is it wealthy in terms of money. Here no one looks down on a scrap car in the driveway or stapling plastic weather sheets over the windows to keep the heat in over the colder months. A piece of decent furniture put by the curb doesn't stay long. We still produce more waste than anyone should, and we consume far more of the world's resources than is responsible, but there remains a tradition that is counter to those realities—a possibility we can work with to move beyond them.

By the afternoon I've shed my sweatshirt and my shoulders are becoming sore. The pile, though clearly diminishing, is still far from gone. I listen to Berry in the resonant and gentle midwestern baritone of Offerman. "We must achieve the character and acquire the skills to live much poorer than we do," Berry says. It's a line from his work that I've printed and posted on my bulletin board. It is the call to the kind of life I long to lead.

The poverty to which Berry calls us is not the poverty of lack, insufficient food and shelter and friendship. Berry means instead the sort of poverty that doesn't pass by a thing of value, the sort that doesn't waste a plate of food because we "don't like leftovers." His is a call to the poverty of self-reliance and neighborliness: "We must waste less. We must do more for ourselves and our neighbors."[2]

This self-reliance is something quite apart from selfishness or a prideful going it alone. It is an ability to live within the means of one's resources and competencies—to make something of what is at hand. It is to live into the gifts of being human and to live, as best as possible, adequately to those gifts. As Berry writes in his essay, "The Agrarian Standard": "Our life of need and work forces us inescapably to use in time things belonging to eternity, and to assign finite values to things already recognized as infinitely valuable. This is a fearful predicament. It calls for prudence, humility, good work, propriety of scale."[3]

---

2. Berry, *World-Ending Fire*, 247.
3. Berry, *World-Ending Fire*, 150.

THOUGHTS WHILE PUSHING A WHEELBARROW

Such virtues are embodied, Berry writes, by those farmers who have taken what the market would deem marginal and been able to make some living from it. "In my various travels, I have seen a number of small homesteads . . . ," Berry writes, "situated on 'land that no one wanted' and yet abundantly productive of food, pleasure, and other goods."[4] This is what living poorer means for Berry—a richness of life drawn from little; the ability to sustain life without the exhaustion of the world. If ours has been a world ravaged by living on more, then its healing means we must live on less.

A few days before the wood chips arrived in my driveway, I'd had a conversation with Claudio Oliver. Claudio is an urban agrarian, living in Curitiba, Brazil. In the midst of the city his community tends lush gardens and keeps goats, chickens, and bees. In their kitchen they make kombucha, bread and pasta, and sell it to their neighbors. There is a video online in which Claudio is answering the question: what is poverty? Poverty, says Claudio, is a lack of friendship.[5] This is poverty in the negative, the kind of lack that leaves those who suffer it depleted rather than self-reliant or wrapped in a network of neighborly care.

When I talk with Claudio he says, "I do not have much money, but I live with great wealth." And yet he says, most of those he encounters are more interested in gaining money than they are wealth: "I offer them wealth, but they only want money." For Claudio, wealth is abundance—it is having food and friends, shelter and conviviality. There are ways to have such things with very little money through an economy of frugality and shared abundance.

To live in this wealth, Claudio takes in what others cast off. Fruit that doesn't look quite right is turned into kombucha, vegetable scraps from the kitchen are made into compost or fed to the chickens, oil that restaurants pay to be hauled off is taken and turned into soap. Where others see waste and death, Claudio's vision is trained to see resurrection. It is this vision that will bring us into the true abundance that an economy of scarce commodities could never achieve.

---

4. Berry, *World-Ending Fire*, 151.
5. RelationalTithe, "What Is Poverty?," August 25, 2008, YouTube video, https://youtu.be/RGSvDvDZnb4.

By the end of the day, as the light faded and family life called me to other work, the pile had been reduced to a small mound I'd have to leave until the morning. Looking around at my garden beds, freshly mulched, the scent of the green wood in the air, I felt a sense of goodness—the fullness of a day of good work. I also felt the rebellion of resourcefulness, like somehow I'd pulled one over on the man. In all of this I felt full of the health of good living, I had sought to live poorer and had become, for a moment, wealthy.

Fear and Grace

I sit before the sun, facing south, each day its path ascending higher in the sky as we tilt toward its light. The winter birds are still here, mostly, but the swallows have begun to arrive—Martins, Tree Swallows, pioneers searching for the cavities in which they will nest. The birds that find their winter home here are now singing their summer songs, readying their voices to set up territories on their nesting ground, a space from which they can support their families. (What if our property boundaries were arranged according to the borders of where our songs could be heard?) The henbit is blooming, playing host to honeybees—both European emigres who have settled into the common life of this place.

I feel in this moment at peace; drawn up into what Wendell Berry has called the "grace of the world." I am party to an immense gift—a favor that is immeasurable. It is grace that is at the center of my life; it is this givenness that marks me out as a creature—reception and offering, both at once. "We live by grace if we live," to quote another line of Berry. And it is grace that was the purpose, the end at which Christ's descent was aimed. He became poor, so that we might become rich.

All of this talk of poverty, of diminishment and self-emptying is within its proper home when grace is the aim, when the generosity of God is at its center. Our poverty, personal and ontological—the fact at the center of our being—is an invitation for reception, an opening for communion. We are impoverished in our very being. We lack in ourselves what is necessary for life unfettered, independent, and yet the God who lacks nothing—the only sufficient reality, came to answer our need. This answer of God's provision for our lack does not end like the static purchase of a product off the shelf. It is an invitation for us to make our own offer; God's gift is an invitation for our own charity.

RETURN

When Paul was writing to the church in Corinth a second time, in a moment of anguish and conflict, Paul was drawn to the poverty of Christ. In his anger, his frustration, his hurt at the rejection from this church that he had gathered and cultivated, Paul recognizes that the only response must be that of Christ's. It is the way of poverty and vulnerable dependence for the sake of love. "For you know the grace of our Lord Jesus Christ," he wrote in his letter, "in that, although he was rich, for your sakes he became poor, so that by his poverty you might be rich" (2 Cor 8:9).

It was Thomas Aquinas, centuries later, who would recognize in these words a statement of our creaturely situation and call. Christ as the Human One, enacted and embodied the life that is proper to all humanity—a poverty for the sake of wealth, shared in the offering of love. As Christopher Franks observes, Aquinas's understanding of "humble vulnerability reflects both the status of the creature before God and the movement of love beyond itself."[1]

To be vulnerable can cause fear. We are without defense in the face of life's fragility. So it is that we are tempted to rebel against our fragility, to secure certainties, even if they are false. Instead of living into our essential fragility, trusting in God for our lives, we look for means by which we can control the variables, fight off the vulnerabilities. "The technological conquest of the natural world has been motivated in large part by a desire to banish fears—that the triumph of human reason may lead to there being nothing left to fear," writes Franks.[2] In reality, though, such a triumph can only be illusory—we cover over our situation or delay it. It is the gift of the world, the gift to which we belong in common, that ultimately suffers.

The choice we have in response to our fears is bankruptcy or frugality, violence or humility. We can live with an appropriate fear, finding refuge in our dependence upon God, or we can seek to overcome our fears through ever more violence, the dispersed schemes of self-preservation. Such schemes manifest themselves in everything from a rationalist clinging to science and technology, hope in an ever forward marching progress, or in "conservative" movements seeking refuge in tradition or the arms of strongmen.

T. S. Eliot saw these contrasting realities as he sought hope amid the dark days of World War II. In his poem "East Coker," Eliot goes to his ancestral homeland, hoping that in the long history of his people he can see

---

1. Franks, *He Became Poor*, 105.
2. Franks, *He Became Poor*, 107–8.

some light for what lies ahead. But Eliot finds the past empty of answers, his elders only mirror his own fear:

> Do not let me hear
> Of the wisdom of old men, but rather of their folly,
> Their fear of fear and frenzy, their fear of possession,
> Of belonging to another, or to others, or to God.[3]

Instead, Eliot is brought to the only ground for hope:

> The only wisdom we can hope to acquire
> Is the wisdom of humility: humility is endless.[4]

There is something promising, Eliot was able to name, in the poverty of our being. It is when we cease to have answers that we can become a vessel awaiting fulfillment.

It is in this humble, vulnerable waiting that fear can be a kind of gift. Aquinas saw fear of the right kind as a gift that delivers hope. When we are at a loss, unable to imagine how to secure our futures, our fear can move us more deeply into attachment to God. Rather than rebelling against fear, seeking to overcome our terror, Aquinas saw the proper human response to fear as a taking refuge in the embrace of God. Like a child, frightened by a nightmare crawling into bed with her parents to feel safe, the human, defenseless against evil, must seek safety in the only place we can really find it—the arms of God. All other possibilities will only perpetuate the very fearful evil that we intended to flee.[5]

Our response, once within that embrace, is one of calm, of hope and gratitude. It is a reality beautifully rendered in the language of Psalm 131:

> I still my soul and make it quiet,
> like a child upon its mother's breast.

This is the proper response to fear in the biblical vision. When we fear the evils around us we don't act, wage war, create plans of power and technological control. Instead, as Psalm 131 goes on to say, we "wait on the Lord." It is in that waiting that we learn to embrace that other biblical call, the most common command in all of Scripture—"fear not, for I am with you."

---

3. Eliot, *Collected Poems*, 185.
4. Eliot, *Collected Poems*, 185.
5. Franks, *He Became Poor*, 108.

It is in our waiting that we learn that what we should fear is not our vulnerability but rather our separation, our alienation from the embrace of God. When fear is focused in this way we are able to answer our givenness with charity, an offering toward others and toward the world. It is the person who has matured in the long experience of loving dependence who is freest to give.

To be able to live with less, to risk vulnerability for the sake of others, is a reality born of the knowledge that we are given, embraced by love. Christ's own poverty, his kenotic self-giving, was made possible because he knew, more than any, the fullness of God's love. As we learn from him that fullness, our response must also be to offer ourselves as gifts that exist in giving. To do so, though it threatens our instincts of preservation, is no risk. We are like children, offering baskets of produce while our parents fill barns with an increasing abundance. God is ready to fill the emptiness we make available.

I watch a single bee upon the henbit, its body covered in the golden grains of pollen. Neither flower nor bee are any value to me in themselves. I won't harvest anything from these flowers and I will never taste the bees' honey. And yet, watching them I am filled with gratitude, a gratitude that draws me toward the desire to make room for more lives like these. I long, for a moment to be poorer, so that I can join in the wealth of the world.

Awe, Awe, Awe

I sat in a strip-mall restaurant, off the highway, windows opening onto the parking lot with trees here and there along the edges trapped in traffic islands. Across from me, at the table, sat Brian. He is a theologian and writer I admire, and I happened to be visiting a town near his home. Would you be up for lunch, I'd asked. He graciously said yes.

We sat, talking—the small talk of common people and connections. Then the food arrived. It can be an awkward moment among religious folk. Is it overly pious to say a prayer here? "May I say grace," Brain offered, resolving the tension. "Yes, of course," I replied. "This is a prayer a nun once taught me," he prefaced the prayer. Then he gestured toward the food with uplifted palms, "Awe," he said. He lifted his hands toward me, "Awe." Finally he lifted his hands toward God, "Awe."

My youngest daughter had not yet learned to speak at the time, but each evening, as we sat at the table for dinner, she would squirm to join in the prayer of thanksgiving. With this prayer of awe I had learned a prayer she could join and lead. "Awe, awe, awe," we began to pray each night in thanksgiving for our food, for one another, for God's ever-flowing grace.

It is an appropriate prayer far beyond its simplicity. Awe is among the most adequate acknowledgments we can have before God's gifts, for "saying grace" can be a fraught reality. Sometimes we bow before a meal made in violence—the extracted produce of abused land, meat cut from an animal whose life was misery. But whatever its origin, the truth of all things, deep down, is one of gift—abused perhaps, exploited and appropriated—but still givenness is beneath it all, a reality to which we can only respond with awe toward the world, awe toward each other, awe before God. It is in that awe that we begin to find the truth of a thing, it is in awe that we begin to find our smallness and make space for even our confusion and suffering.

Awe can also be a call to confession. It can be the acknowledgment that we have tried to control the world; it can be a away of saying that despite our exploitation of the earth, our enclosure of God's gifts within the commodities of exchange, there is still a remainder we haven't captured and consumed, a gift available despite us—grace after all.

Thanksgiving is often inhibited by our pain, the suffering of our lives that hides the gift of the world under the cloak of despair. But awe, here too, is an opening toward grace. In the book of Job, when its eponymous hero finally turns to God and asks the cause of all his suffering, the response is awe. God gives no answer other than a gesture toward the wild world that serves no human purpose—the ravens fed by God's hand, the rains that come in the desert where no human beings live. To turn to awe is to say like Job, "I am dust and ashes" before the wonder of God, the wonder of creation, the wonder in which our pain becomes a drop in the wideness of God's mercy. Awe, awe, awe.

Among the Inuit, a culture remarkable for its lack of anger, children are redirected from their rage with awe. An angry child is brought outside, shown something beautiful, and calmed by the perspective of finding oneself beneath a starry night or before a blazing flower. Awe is the path toward thanksgiving, of finding our place in the world and being grateful that we are part of it, even for a moment.[1]

In *The Cloud of Unknowing*, a fourteenth-century work of mysticism, the anonymous author instructs the reader to find a different path toward humility than that gained by the meditation upon one's sins. Instead, the author makes an appeal to awe—awe at God's excellence:

> ... choose to be humbled by the wonderful height and excellence of God, who is perfect, rather than by your own sinfulness, which is imperfect; that is to say, see that you give special regard to God's excellence rather than your own sinfulness. For to those who have perfect humility, nothing shall be lacking, either in body or in spirit; because they have God, in whom is all plenty; and whoever has him ... needs nothing else in this life.[2]

Anger comes when our way is violated; when we see injustice in the world and feel no power to stop it. Anger and despair and dissatisfaction come when our will is burdened, we attempt to be Atlas, keeping the world aloft. We try to be gods, aligning the world to our whims and frustrated

1. Doucleff, *Hunt, Gather, Parent*, 176–77.
2. Anonymous, *Cloud of Unknowing*, 48.

when others do not fall in line. But awe is an entrance to peace, to the gentle power of grace. When we are caught up in awe, we can see the truth that we are finite, a shutter snap in the cosmic timeline, and yet we are loved, remembered, held in the embrace of God's gifts. It is in awe that we can experience *kairos*, the time of God's redeeming action, overwhelming the march of *chronos*, the time of ticking clocks.

To discover that we are small is to enter the grace of the world, our hands outstretched like a child who can't yet speak and yet wants to say grace: awe, awe, awe. It is with awe that we discover we have all we need. The challenge is how we receive that gift, how we learn to recognize what has already been given.

We Have What We Need

> . . . And we pray, not
> for new earth or heaven, but to be
> quiet in heart, and in eye,
> clear. What we need is here.
>
> WENDELL BERRY, "THE WILD GEESE"

I wander the aisles of Lowe's, the pedometer in my watch clicking a quarter mile of steps, as I walk across the buffed concrete. For all the millions of products, the nexus of oil and steel, the confluence of global manufacturing, I can't find what I'm looking for. Milling about, there are employees with vests, "May I help you?" emblazoned on their backs. When they turn around, their faces don't repeat the question. I ask anyway, and one after another has no clue what I'm talking about. "Excuse me," I say with my typical Southern deference, "can you tell me where I can find hardware cloth?" What I'd taken to be a common construction material has evidently never been encountered by anyone on staff. Finally, still puzzled, one man standing beside a shelf full of screws suggests I try the garden center.

I walk another quarter mile from the lumber section through the sliding glass double doors, through the hanging plastic of the indoor plant greenhouse, and out to the open-air aisles of the garden center. There are pallets of river gravel, peet-moss, phosphorous amendments, and nitrogen pellets. The only compost on sale is cow manure "compost," likely processed from a feedlot like the one I once passed outside Amarillo, Texas, the stench sensed long before the sight of the steers, shoulder to shoulder in their own shit.

To the right of the compost there were bags of "top soil." I knew a farmer once who'd taken to selling his top soil, along with sand from the river at the edge of his fields. "I make more selling my soil than anything I can grow out of it," he said in a despairing boast. The dirt in these bags came from somewhere—a river-built valley, a prairie-built plain. Everything in these bays and bags came from somewhere: the peet-moss was mined from a boreal bog; the river gravel pulled from a stream.

All of these bags, mined and manufactured, synthesized and packaged, were on sale to fill a need. If I just bought three bags of X for $16.99 then all would be well with my yard. I was traveling those aisles with a different end in mind, the hope that I already have what is necessary.

Eventually, I found my hardware cloth, clearly labeled alongside the chicken wire, midway up a steel-framed rack. It came from somewhere too, mined and manufactured, and perhaps I could do better. But my hope was that with this purchase I'd be gaining a tool for work, rather than a product for consumption. With this tool I'd be entering a different economy—one that moves in ever greater circles of givenness.

The wire now sits in the back corner of my yard, a cylinder held together by bungee cords. Around the top there is a blue tarp, a few fall leaves settled in its crease. Inside the wire there is a mix of organic matter—wood chips and cardboard boxes, grass clippings, the stems and peels left over after our meals, coffee grounds and a bucket of beer mash from a local brewery. I'd mixed it all together, watered it until I could squeeze a few drops from a handful, and let the microbes get to work. The thermometer whose disk extends from the side of the wire reached 170 degrees Fahrenheit, staying there for a couple of days. When it dropped, I'd mix it all again, until every part of the pile had been through the hot center—killing off the pathogenic microbes and weed seeds. Now it is cool, settled into the slower pattern of decay with the white filaments of fungi working their way through, dissolving the debris with their tangled bodies. In the spring I'll spread it across my gardens, an inoculation to cultivate the life of the soil.

This composting process is one I'd learned from Elaine Ingham, a pioneering soil scientist who introduced many practitioners to the web of soil life. With a growing following of regenerative farmers and ecologically minded gardeners interested in her work, she formed her own Soil Food Web school, leaving the university world behind. I'd been enrolled for several months in the "Introduction to the Soil Food Web" course, watching hour upon hour of videos with Dr. Elaine Ingham explaining every aspect of life in the soil and the tools we have to cultivate it. At the heart of it all, compost is key, but it needs to be the right kind of compost, alive with the kinds of organisms that help build soil and support plants, the aerobic microbes that cycle oxygen, capturing CO_2 rather than releasing methane.

In one of the early lessons of her introductory course, Ingham offered a startling fact for anyone who has sent off a soil test to a lab: most soils in the world have all of the chemical elements needed to support life. As botanists and any good gardener knows, there are three major elements, unique atoms on the periodic table, needed for plants to grow—nitrogen, phosphorous, and potassium—known by their periodic table symbols as N-P-K. Different ratios are necessary, but each is needed for the overall health of the plant. In addition, there are dozens of other micronutrients that are important for plant metabolism and ultimately animal health too.

Much of the work of gardening from the perspective of the industrial model is adding the chemicals necessary to bring the soil into balance—the right amount of N-P-K along with achieving the proper pH for what you are trying to grow. And so, depending on one's bent, gardeners buy manure high in nitrogen, blood meal high in potassium, bone meal high in phosphorous; or "Miracle Grow," a chemically synthesized mix of it all. For the pH, there's lime to raise the soil toward base or sulfur to lower it toward the acidic side.

But what if none of this was necessary? What if instead of worrying about chemistry we concerned ourselves with community—gathering the life necessary for the circle of gifts, the webs of reciprocity at work in the soil?

That there is another way becomes clear when we take nature as our measure, as we humbly look to what the world does without us. Like the lilies of the field that neither sow nor reap, a mature forest or grassland is able to cultivate an abundance of life without any bags of pelletized nitrogen. And while no forest I know of is able to mine a distant hillside for lime, the appropriate soil pH is achieved nonetheless. When we follow the patterns of the given world, we can begin to re-examine the shape of our agriculture and ask again what builds the fertility that leads to flourishing.

These are questions Sir Albert Howard asked at the beginning of chemical agriculture just after the start of the twentieth century. In 1909 Fritz Haber discovered how to fix nitrogen—taking what had been a hard to handle gas and making it available for use in agricultural fields. He won the Nobel Peace Prize for the work, for it saved many from starvation (Haber would go on to be convicted of war crimes, but that's another story). Sir Albert Howard, however, was unconvinced that this chemical approach was

We Have What We Need

the best way to achieve healthy food. He understood, from a variety of trials as a researcher in India, that the earth had its own way of building fertility.

Though he didn't yet have the tools to understand all of the biological processes at play, he saw that nature used cycles of organic matter to replenish its needs without synthetic inputs. The work of a farmer, in Howard's understanding, was to follow the patterns of nature and build soil humus. The way he learned to achieve this, following some practices he gleaned from indigenous farmers in India, was to make compost. While Howard saw that compost had a tremendous effect on soil fertility he didn't understand, at least in a scientific way, why it worked as it did. It was left to later researchers like Ingham to recognize what compost does for the soil and the microscopic life that makes it possible.

According to Ingham, geologists have found that most of the world's soils contain plenty of nitrogen, phosphorous, and potassium, along with a host of other "trace" elements necessary for healthy plants. Even where the soil is lacking, the air itself is chock-full of nitrogen waiting to be "fixed" in the soil. What's necessary, then, isn't obtaining these elements. The challenge is making them accessible to the life processes of living things, "bioavailable" in the language of science. It's like having a pantry full of canned food and no can-opener: what's needed to open the food in the pantry is the soil food web—a complex network of life made up of bacteria and fungi at its base and then organisms like protozoa, nematodes, and micro-arthropods who feed on them. Through their respiration and digestion, these organisms unlock the available nutrients in the soil. What's more, they do it in cooperation with plants that offer various foods to draw in the organisms necessary for their needs. These plants can also control the pH around their root systems, making all of the worry over lime and sulfur an unnecessary step in many cases.

All of these realities point to the truth that "what we need is here." We have already received the necessary gifts; they are graces that invite us into the circle of life, a circle whose dance we must learn. The gifts given in soil, free from the necessity of the products and commercial inputs, are offered without our need to earn them. But just as they are given without our earning them, we must learn to receive them. As the philosopher Dallas Willard has put it, "Grace is opposed to earning, not to effort. And *it is well-directed, decisive and sustained effort that is the key to the keys of the kingdom and to the life of restful power . . . that those keys can open to us*" (emphasis his).[1] Like a character in a fairy tale who receives a magic object and is then humbled into its appropriate use, we need to learn how to live with what we've been given and work with its power within our limits, turning it toward the restful power of grace that is at home in the reign of God. What we must acquire is not a product, but the skills for our inevitable and necessary use of the world.

---

1. Willard, *Great Omission*, 34.

Skill

I pull back the blue tarp and lean over the wire edge, reaching down into the pile. It gives easily to my push, releasing the aroma of earth. The smell evokes backpacking trips to the Ozark mountains, where campsites are made not in predetermined places with gravel pads and iron fire grates, but at the place exhaustion meets even ground and a stream runs nearby. In those places we sit and sleep on the earth, smelling the slow rot, the new beginnings of death begetting life. That smell is the scent of humus; it is the smell of a compost pile that is working as it should. Here there are no longer the distinguishable and varied inputs of leaves and straw, food scraps and coffee grounds. All has been transformed into a new body of dark earth.

I pull up a handful, a moist sponge between my fingers, and place it in a bag, working it to break apart the clumps as I walk, undoing the structures glued together through the construction of microbes. On my kitchen table I have a graduated test tube, a microscope, slides and pipettes. I pour a little of the compost into the tube, tapping it until I have one milliliter. Over the compost I pour filtered water until the bottom curve of the viscous line evens out at five milliliters. I screw on the blue top and gently rock the mix back and forth, suspending the compost in the water to make a dark brown tea. When the tube is open again, I plunge a pipette down beneath the layer of organic matter floating to the top and draw up a few drops of water, ready for the slide.

One drop of dirty water spreads beneath the slip as I place the slide between the calipers of the microscope platform. I focus the light, dialing the platform up and down until a sharp image appears, magnified at 200x. I see a teeming mass of bacteria in the hundreds of thousands—all vibrating through the liquid, clusters congregated around the fragments of organic matter. Almost as soon as I achieve my focus, the water begins to move, bacteria displaced by the flow. A nematode comes into view, wriggling snake-like through the sample. It is transparent and inside the long tube of its body are the dark spots of bacteria—the remnants of its microbial feast. I watch the nematode as it opens its mouth, gobbling bacteria as it goes. This is how the nitrogen-rich bodies of bacteria turn into plant-available nutrients; this is how the soil food web makes humus.

I move on, rolling the platform up and down, scanning for what else is here in this drop of compost. I see a small blob, moving frenetically around the edge of a piece of "micro-aggregate," a tiny fragment of sand. This is a protozoa, a single-celled predator, ripping free the bacteria that have glued themselves to the particle's surface. A little to the left, I see another species of protozoa, working a field of bacteria so thick in number I couldn't begin to count them. Predators are good. Like lions on the savannah or eagles on a lake's edge, they mark a working cascade of energy.

Continuing my scan I find bits of what appears to be a microscopic stick. It's a fragment of fungal hyphae—a golden, toast-like brown—the mark of fulvic and humic acids. Along its length the width remains even, and spaced in regular increments are the walls of septum. This hyphae belongs to a mycorrhizal fungus that's working through the pile, eating the woodchips and leaves, breaking apart the carbons in the compost. It's a beneficial fungus, the kind I'm hoping to cultivate, the kind that will develop relationships with plants, exchanging nutrients with them through their roots and serving as a network of communication.

Looking down through the lens, I feel something. It is not pride, but a kind of satisfaction. I didn't create anything here, I didn't manufacture the life working in this compost pile, but I played a role, I facilitated a process by which the soil food web came into its fullness. In that small drop of dirty water was evidence that my compost is working. It is growing life, beneficial life, that will help heal the soil. In this compost, I'd taken something I've been given and received it with skill.

How do we live into the grace of the world? How do we flourish, knowing our limits, accepting our ignorance? The aim isn't mastery, but an ever more adequate and appropriate reception of our given lives within the given world.

Adequate because we continue to live under the guidance of the fundamental truth of our lives—that we are creatures who are both finite and limited in our capacities to understand. Humility protects us from

Skill

the presumption of any perfect action or complete acquisition of the truth; it keeps our virtue human rather than making virtue into a means of transcendence.

What we can find at the end of all our efforts is not the truth in full, but an adequate understanding of it. What we can do, at best, is not all that is needed, but enough for our finite moment. We can get better, make our lives more adequate to the reality of the world, but like Zeno and his paradox where the distance can always be halved, we'll never arrive, nor should we expect to reach any ultimate endpoint. All those cliches about the journey not the destination reflect a truth here—part of any finite life is the continued journey of approach.

Skill is what enables us to increase our adequacy to the world and turn it toward appropriate action. Appropriate because we acknowledge that there are times when we have access to powers that enable us to work beyond our limits, beyond what is proper to care. In such cases we step over the boundaries of what is ours, the gifts we've been given for which we can properly exercise affection and kindness in our work. Skill, real skill, is what keeps us grounded in the places where appropriate care can be exercised.

James Rebanks, in his memoir, *Pastoral Song*, gives voice to the challenge of appropriate action and the way that virtue can guide it. Pressured by the changing economics of farming, Rebanks recounts how his family began to utilize larger tractors and pesticides. It was a move that Rebanks's grandfather despised:

> my grandfather had oozed contempt for tractors. He used them, and the machinery that came with them, but he didn't like what they did to us, because the moment we stepped up onto them, we raised ourselves from the earth, no longer touching it, smelling it, feeling it. That sensory contact was the essence of knowing the land . . . He thought machine work was of a lower order of importance than working with animals or with your hands. Any fool could drive a tractor around and around a field.[1]

In the contempt of Rebanks's grandfather for machine work, we see a key aspect of skilled labor—it requires intelligence, an aptitude of mind, but also a broader wisdom of the body. A skilled farmer is attentive to the reality of the land and animals. Though it may not be articulable, or even expressible in words, a skilled farmer can often see when a ewe is about to give birth, know when something is unhealthy in a patch of pasture, or even

1. Rebanks, *Pastoral Song*, 117.

sense when the weather is about to make a change. Skill is a reality of the soul in which the mental, bodily, spiritual, ecological, and social realities of the self come together. From an athlete to a farmer to a house framer—a skilled person is one who is able to be fully engaged, through the totality of the self, in a particular kind of work.

To develop the skills adequate to receiving the gifts that we have been given, to honor the value of the world, requires both attention and failure. Skill, in fact, could be described as an ever more acute training in attention and the power adequate to address and anticipate our failures. Most people, for instance, go about with some vague sense that there are birds around. They may know a robin, a cardinal, a chickadee, but they have simply no idea that there may be more than thirty species around them at any one time or that in certain places and seasons, they could see well over a hundred species in a day. But for a birder, a person who has carefully trained her attention to birds over time, each particular species stands out. This skill is born of attention and then reinforces it in a circle—the more attentive the more skilled; and the more skilled the better the quality of attention.

Failure also has a role to play in the development of skill. I remember a shop class teacher telling about learning to weld when he was a student. Each person in his class had to choose a community project for their final shop class grade. He decided that he was going to repair an old iron fence at a local cemetery. Though he had only limited welding experience, he knew enough to feel like this project was achievable. The problem was that he had never fused two different kinds of metal and that is what he was attempting to do. Before he started, his shop class teacher gave him a welding book and told him to read it. Overconfident, the boy attempted the weld without reading. When he tried to join the metals they popped and shattered. The shop class teacher sat at his desk laughing. The boy had failed and was now ready to learn. The teacher told him again to look at the book, and this time the student did, learning the perils and correct methods of fusing two different kinds of metals.

This anecdote points to an important aspect of the development of skill. If we are going to work in the world then we are going to fail. Such failure not only helps to put us in our place, but also helps us mature our skills with wisdom. To master a thing without failure is flirting with hubris. Our hope should not be the avoidance of failure, but to fail early, often, and clearly enough that we can hone our skill over time.

Skill

Again, to go to the birding example, many new birders want to save themselves embarrassment by not identifying a bird that could be difficult. But birders who try out an identification can be corrected with helpful feedback, enabling them to learn the subtle signs by which different species are distinguished. Even experienced birders make bad calls, but usually they recognize that they may be wrong. I often see good birders advertise a "possible" rare bird with all the caveats. They risk failure on the chance they may be right and have found something extraordinary. Either way, other birders will help sort out the subtleties.

Humility helps to discipline our failures by expecting them. We know that there is always more to learn, much that we don't know, and we recognize that we won't ever achieve complete mastery. Pride comes when we assume perfectibility, when our growth in a skill becomes an attempt to totalize it. Skills must always be practiced within the bounds of propriety—an expectation of failure. For we will fail, eventually, and it is important that failure does as little damage as possible, that it is open to healing and repair. A failed garden can be remedied the next year; a nuclear meltdown is beyond repair on any human time scale.

"[O]ur capacity to fail makes us what we are," writes the philosopher Costica Bratadan, "our being as essentially failing creatures lies at the root of any aspiration."[2] This capacity comes from our inevitable limits—our ignorance, our weakness, our mortality. To be human, in Bratadan's view, is to learn to live into these realities, and failure can help us with this learning as almost nothing else can. And yet, to realize this truth is also to find meaning and peace. When we eventually come to terms with the reality that we are finite, that we will die, we are able to accept the truth by which we find freedom.

---

2. Bradatan, "In Praise of Failure," para. 15.

The Bread of Heaven

When I was first apprenticing in agriculture, I met a wheat farmer and sheep rancher from Western Oklahoma named Kim Barker. An avid reader, he told me that if I wanted to learn how to farm I should go to used bookstores and antique shops, searching for agriculture texts that were written before the rise of synthetic fertilizers and pesticides. "The old books tell you how to do things," Kim said, "while the new ones only tell you what to buy."

That is how, one day, I found myself digging through a dumpster. I wasn't foraging for day-old sushi or expired dairy (though I admire the "freegans" whose stomachs can handle such things). Instead, this dumpster belonged to the Conway County Library where a number of "outdated books" had just been culled. Among them were several farming books of just the sort for which Kim told me to look. The best was a slim volume with a yellow cover, the dust jacket wrapped with the usual plastic of a library book. It was Andre Voison's *Fertilizer Application*.

Voison was working at the point when synthetic nitrogen was making its way from the bomb factories of World War II to the farm fields of Europe and America. And though not opposed to these fertilizers, per se, he came to see that they were not a simple net positive. As his research showed: applying large amounts of synthetic nitrogen, potassium, and phosphorus resulted in other important nutrients in the soil beginning to disappear.

Riboflavin, Voison argued, could be diminished in soils supplemented with synthetic fertilizer. Vegetables then grown from that soil would lack sufficient amounts of this protective nutrient. The result, he believed, would be wide-spread diseases of malnourishment among those with more than enough to eat.

Contemporary research has borne out Voison's vision. In England, the Broadbalk research station has continually measured nutrient levels in wheat since 1843. What they've found is that since the introduction of modern wheat in 1968 the content of zinc, iron, copper, magnesium, phosphorus, manganese, sulfur, and calcium has plummeted 18 to 29 percent. While wheat became more abundant, the bread made from it became far less nourishing.

I thought of this reality as I read what's known as the "bread of life discourse" found in chapter 6 of the Gospel of John. There Jesus, having just fed over 5,000 people with a couple of loaves and fishes, begins to teach that he is "the bread of life" that comes down from heaven. "Your ancestors ate manna in the wilderness and they died," he teaches. "I am the living bread that came down from heaven. Whoever eats this bread will live forever, and the bread that I will give for the life of the world is my flesh" (v. 51).

The Gospel of John, of course, was written well before synthetic fertilizers and modern wheat strains. Most people lived, more or less, on a bread that was rich and nutritious, with grains grown from soils teeming with the microbes that sustain plant life. And yet, the difference between modern and ancient wheat offers us insight into the bread of the ancestors and the living bread that Jesus gives. It is a difference of direction and relationship; fast food on the way to something else or a feast at which we linger.

To help his hearers understand what he is offering, Jesus points them back to one of the great miracles of the Bible—the giving of manna in the wilderness. Manna was God's life-sustaining answer to Israel's need during the Exodus from Egypt. But this miraculous bread that helped the people of Israel find their freedom, was always meant to be only an expression of the true source of Israel's sustenance—their abiding relationship with the living God.

The problem, then as now, is that the people paid no attention to the deeper source of their nourishment. Once they ate the manna, they forgot all about continuing to trust in God's provision and love. As Psalm 78 recounts the story:

> In spite of all this they still sinned;
>   they did not believe in his wonders.
> So he made their days vanish like a breath,
>   and their years in terror. (78:32–33)

This episode was a critical one in Israel's story. No fewer than three Psalms recount Israel's refusal to be satisfied with God's gift of manna, and Jesus's hearers would have known these verses by memory. When he tells them in a key passage of his sermon that their ancestors ate the manna in the wilderness and died, Jesus is not offering anything that would have been news to his audience. The people of God were always facing the same old challenge—to be consumers of God's gifts or participants in God's abiding life? Jesus's difficult teaching is that they were once again taking God's gifts for their own selfish ends, living as users of God's provision rather than sharers in his life.

※

Much of industrial agriculture follows the pattern of the strip-mine. It extracts but does not replenish. And this pattern of consumption without return is one that is pervasive in our society, even our religion. We are hungry and God has spread a perpetual feast before us. But we opt instead for a cheap substitute, grabbing a bite on the way to the rest of our lives, wondering as Psalm 78 puts it, why we "can't stop [our] craving even though the food is still in [our] mouths" (v. 30).

Jesus, in John's Gospel, offers a different way, one that goes back to God's gift of nourishment in his covenant with Israel. Jesus is calling for us to move away from the patterns of consumption that will only leave us depleted, however much we eat, and to instead participate in the continuous energy available from the everlasting life of God. We move to this participation by way of return and relationship.

A contemporary of Andre Voison was Sir Albert Howard. In his important book, *The Soil and Health*, Howard wrote that many of our ecological problems are a "punishment meted out by Mother Nature for adopting methods of agriculture which are not in accordance with Nature's law of return."[1] The law of return is essentially the law of the gift. Gifts are not things we receive and deposit, storing them away. For gifts to be true gifts they must be circulated, not in exchange but in reciprocity. When we receive the gift of good food from soil, our response should be to return life to the soil with mulch and compost. And the same pattern holds in our life of faith. God is a host who invites us to come, share a meal, to eat together in the continual conversation of love. It is not something we pay for and consume, but rather a relationship we enter through the circle of God's grace. The Eucharist, when it is eaten as a meal of thanksgiving, is a sign of that sharing and gift, but it is not one we can abide in alone.

Good food is always the result of life together. As Sir Albert Howard wrote: "the problems of the farm and garden are biological rather than

1. Howard, *Soil and Health*, xxv.

chemical."[2] In the industrial model the soil becomes little more than a medium of inputs for agricultural outputs, exchange rather than reciprocity. But good, sustaining soil—the kind that provides rich and nutritious food—is made through an ongoing community of living relationship. From fungi to protozoa, moles to microbes, good soil is the common ground of a common life. And this too is a truth of our abiding in Christ. It is through the return of our thanksgiving and the life of relationship that we become participants in the divine, joining in the community gathered at the banquet to which God is always calling us. It is a reality, like any good loaf of bread, in which we find our nourishment together.

In seminary, I occasionally baked bread for our Eucharists. There was a rotation, and we were guided only by a common recipe. When it came my turn, I went to a specialty store and bought flour milled from an ancient kind of wheat, the Einkorne that likely grew on the Palestinian plains of the Jesus's day. The wheat was grown by farmers following the renewing patterns pioneered by Voison and Howard, a way of agriculture that focused on sustaining the community of life beneath the ground. I mixed the wheat with olive oil, sourced from a Palestinian cooperative of farmers not far from Bethlehem. At the end of mixing, I sweetened the dough with a bit of honey from a nearby farm in the Shenandoah Valley. When we received it together, during the eucharistic meal, little bits torn and given, it was a gathering of life and care, of return and relationship. And as we ate the wheat, born of so much life, we were opened to the nourishment of the one whose flesh is true bread and blood is true drink. It was a sign of the meal to which we are invited, the table that God set before us saying, "come and stay, eat and be satisfied."

---

2. Howard, *Soil and Health*, xxv.

Affluence and Abundance

I followed the old ATV track, the shale laden with mud, gullied out in spots, quartz exposed and shining white like porcelain beneath. Here and there along the road, I'd encounter a band of chickadees and titmice, foraging among the fall leaves that were still green beneath the late September sun. I paused to see if there was a silent warbler in their midst, making its way south. I didn't linger long. My aim was the ridgeline above, "Rattlesnake Ridge," known for hosting all three Arkansas species of its eponymous reptiles. I would count it luck to find one, having only encountered one rattler in all my years in the woods of Arkansas. It was a cool enough day that most would be slow moving, but perhaps that very cool would draw them out to the warm open spaces on the rocks. Still, I was here not for what lay on the ground, but for what was in the sky—the hawks and eagles, falcons and vultures making their way to their wintering grounds.

Once on the ridge, I picked my way west along the boulders, looking down on the lake that supplies our local water—a dammed river that forms a reservoir, etched among the hills like a jigsaw piece, a few small islands in its midst. Though there are no natural lakes here, it has become the winter home to loons and rafts of ducks. Last year, along its edge, I'd watched a Bald Eagle swim to shore, its wings outstretched as it paddled, drowning a duck beneath the water as it swam. It was greeted by its mate on the beach, where the two butchered the bird together. Today the eagles, some resident, some migrants, are plentiful—soaring with all the regal power that has made them the go-to emblem of empires—hunting, scavenging, stealing prey from smaller raptors.

As I walked along the ridge, few trees grew among the rocks, the winds too strong and the soil too shallow. Instead, there were varied shrubs, all laden with fruit—timed to this fall season of feasting before the bare months of winter. Summer has its wealth, but fall has a special sort of abundance in the temperate wild. The ground was gorged with acorns, the hickories were filled with scolding squirrels, their tails wrapped over their backs as they chewed through the tough shells. In sunny places, long grasses were going to seed. I watched as one was stripped expertly by a sparrow, head cocked to the side, working her beak and tongue along the stalk.

Most abundant on the ridge were the American Beautyberries, their fruit bunched in almost neon purple. I picked them as I passed, drawing my hand along a cluster. The berries were slightly sweet, with a distinct spicy flavor. Lower to the ground, huckleberries were fruiting—a bit plainer in flavor, their fruit resembling blueberries in shape but without their sweetness. I gathered these too as I walked, eating handfuls.

Halfway along the ridge I found a larger shrub, with oak-like leaves and large berries, dark and round like olives. When I tasted them they were sweet, a biological confirmation that they were likely edible. I took a picture and sent it to a botanist friend who confirmed that this was a Gum Bumelia shrub.

Eventually, I came to an outcropping, sandstone shaded by a Post Oak just down the ridge. There was a sumac by the flat rock where I sat, and as I scanned the northern sky I would grab handfuls of its berries, pouring the velvety clusters into my mouth. They have a lemon flavor and are used as a spice for many Middle Eastern dishes—one of those genera that have nearly global natural distribution. Whenever I'd pick a handful, my hands would be covered with an oily residue, a sign of their high fat content—heart protective like olive oil.

On that day, one I'd made free of obligations, I could not help but feel the abundance of the world and its giftedness. I was here to watch birds, to be in nature in the passive way of an observer—the typical urbanite's relationship with the natural world. But even in my slight knowledge of natural edibles, I'd found a feast that put me in a different relationship with the world around me. I had found myself at a banquet, uninvited but welcomed anyway, one guest among many.

※

I had come to the ridge feeling the burdens of work, of family life, of all of the logistics and bureaucracies of modern life. My hike was an attempt to step away from that, to return to myself through the awe of the world. Ever since I was a teenager, hawk-watching during the fall migration has been a seasonal meditation. In high school I would watch the northern sky almost every afternoon, taking a lawn chair to the mountain top field near our home. I'd just stare at the horizon, waiting for what might come. Some days, it would be a group of vultures, teetering on the wind for miles. Other days, when the cumulous clouds rose in towering columns and a cold front pushed south, there would be hundreds of broad-winged hawks riding the thermals of heat in a twisting vortex. Amid the hawks I'd see monarch butterflies in the hundreds, making their own migration—startlingly fragile creatures that were nonetheless journeying a distance farther than that traveled by most people I knew.

"Consider the birds of the air," Jesus taught on his own mountain top. I've never traveled to Israel, but I want to go someday. To see the holy sites, sure. I believe in Incarnation and place and the way the holy can be embodied in the particular. I want to see the geography of all those stories I've read for so many years. But even if the Bible was set in some other place, I'd want to go to Israel for the fall migration of hawks. Israel is a place like Veracruz, Mexico—a funnel where raptors skirt the water, taking an overland route from Europe to Africa.

What if Jesus was there on the mountain as migrating birds were passing overhead—"consider the birds of the air, they neither sow nor reap." They do not stand back from the landscape, planning its cultivation, no. Instead, they are in it, living with it and from it. I know what Jesus means, but in reality, the birds do sow and they do reap. Birds even form the landscapes around them in drastic ways. Hawks in Australia have been known to pick up burning branches from a wildfire and drop them in unburned fields, setting them aflame to then feast on the fleeing rodents. More commonly birds spending time in one place slowly change it to support their life, concentrating the seeds of their favorite foods through the seed bombs of their excrement.

I planted an elderberry in my yard. Now elderberries spring up in any un-mown corner because the birds have spread its seeds. The same goes for mulberries and wild cherry, hackberries, and the invasive privet I try to dig out, but birds love to eat. Blue Jays plant more actively, storing acorns in the soil with only a halfhearted hope of recovering each one. Do they know they are planting, cultivating more of the acorns they feast on, the oak leaves that attract the myriad caterpillars they love? I cannot say, but they are planting nonetheless and so extending the possibilities of their life and livelihood. It is all sowing but sowing without worry. They reap but not with any sense of responsibility for the return, prodigal in their planting. The birds live as a link in the chain of abundance—"given lives in a given world."

What Jesus recommends as our attitude to the world is not agricultural in the traditional sense. Instead, he commends the attitude of a forager, a hunter and gatherer. As varied studies of hunter-gatherer societies have shown, the relationships of hunter-gatherers, both ancient and modern, is rarely a pristine life that is lived in an untouched "wild." Instead, most hunter-gatherer societies shape their landscapes through tending and cultivating the givens of their world, by utilizing fire to clear underbrush or encouraging edible plants over those that are poisonous. Just as weekend deer hunters create spaces to attract their prey, so hunter-gatherers often "manage" wildlife. As M. Kat Anderson traces in her book, *Tending the Wild: Native American Knowledge and the Management of California's Natural Resources*, the pristine wilderness that was so celebrated by John Muir as a cathedral made without human hands, was in fact the result of millennia of management by the very native people Muir disdained.[1]

What is different about this tended wild and the agricultural attitudes of those who "sow and reap" is the control of the givens. A cattle rancher is responsible for the health of her cow from birth to death, utilizing an animal bred for maximal human benefit. But that cow is also totally dependent upon human management, unable to survive without it. A hunter-gatherer works in a less controlling way to encourage the benefit of prey animals and foods, but leaves them ultimately independent. It is a cultivation of the conditions for abundant life rather than the control of that life. Such a cultivation of the pattern of creation's gifts is reflected in the economy of manna.

Egypt was one of the early agricultural societies that centralized power through the storage of grains. It had abundance in surplus, but it was a manufactured abundance, not of the wild givens but of constant labor and control. Working from the starting place of the good soils of the Nile plain, Egypt formed a way of life that relied on stored food rather than seasonal patterns of life. This created a way of relating to the world that was no longer rooted in a sense of its essential goodness and abundance. Food was not what was accepted from the good earth, but instead became the produce of long seasonal labors and engineering. The control of land, people, pests,

---

1. Anderson, *Tending the Wild*, 108–9.

and crops all became central to those efforts, and Israel found itself caught in the midst of that reality.

There is little evidence outside of the Bible that the Israelites were slaves in Egypt. Does this falsify the biblical accounts? Instead, it may shine a light on the formational narrative of Israel's self-understanding. As Claudio Oliver once put it to me, though the Israelites were not slaves in the chattel sense, they were captive to the exploitation of their limited options. Oliver compares the people of Israel to Central American undocumented laborers working in the United States. They were essential to the ongoing economy of the empire, and they were made dependent upon it, yet they were always kept off kilter so their exploitation could be continued.

The people of Israel learned that they were slaves by being liberated—a freedom that was made through manna, the food that could not be stored. Manna, and wild quail dropped right in their midst, came at a time when the people of Israel were longing to return to Egypt and the security it provided. In the story of the exodus we have the perennial story of civilization—freedom versus security. But of course, as we know from that story, it is a false sense of security. All Empires exhaust themselves and the most sustained communities of life have not been formed around settled agriculture. It was that lesson that God wanted to teach Israel—a trust in him and the goodness of creation that he provided. It would be an important lesson because manna and its patterns were to discipline the settled agriculture that would emerge in Israel once it was "settled" in the promised land—an agriculture that was to reflect both serving and preserving the soil.

The promised land, the people of Israel were to always understand, was not theirs. It belonged to God, just as the wilds belonged to God. Their tenure on the land was conditional upon the way they conducted their life upon it—how they lived in relationship with God, the earth, and their neighbors. This view of land tenure was in deep contrast to the sort of land relationship that typically arises in settled agricultural societies. The people of Israel, though they became agricultural, were to relate to the land with a vision more akin to that of hunter-gatherers.

~

The anthropologist James Suzman has spent his life studying the Ju/'hoansi people of the Kalahari. Until recently, the Ju/'hoansi were mostly hunter-gatherers, carrying on a culture in that landscape that has existed in a sustained way for thousands of years. Despite the harshness of the landscape, the Ju/'hoansi have lived with plenty, a situation Suzman has called "affluence without abundance."

In an interview with the journalist Ezra Klein, Suzman explored the difference in attitude between agriculturalists and hunter-gatherers. As Suzman explained, "hunter-gatherers viewed their environments as inherently provident, as almost generous, as something which gave [to] them." With farming, he goes on to explain, "you have to view your environment as only potentially provident. For it to be provident, you have to invest your labor into it."[2]

This assessment is strikingly similar to the Enlightenment philosopher John Locke's attempt to defend the acquisition of property. For Locke, the gifts of God were essentially raw material, without given value. They were made valuable only by the mixing of our labors with the land, a mixing that could include a transfer of our labors through money. It was in this way that Locke justified the ownership of the land and the taking of it from the indigenous people in colonial states. Because they were not "adding value," or making use of the land, they were wasting it and had no title to it.

Of course, as we have seen, indigenous peoples did very much use the land. But not in the agricultural sense and thus not in the sense that makes long-term property ownership important. It is a difference that has as much to do with a sense of time as of place. As Suzman explains the reality of agricultural societies, "the problem with not being able to meet your immediate needs is those future rewards are rewards that are then stored and used to sustain you over the next agricultural cycle. So farmers found themselves locked into this kind of circular time, this process where they invested their labor into the land. And the land, in effect, gave them a return at some point in the future. And this, of course, changed not only the relationship with land because the land became something—if you worked that land, you had some kind of claim of ownership. So it changed their notions of territoriality and ownership."[3]

This changed sense of ownership led to a changed vision of the giftedness of creation and led, with time, to an ever increasing apparatus of security, including the defense of one's stored wealth. It is against this mode that Jesus is directing us, even if we plant and sow. It is through this welcoming of God's gifts that we are able to envision the world not through scarcity and defensiveness, but through abundance and dependence upon

2. Klein, "Ezra Klein Interviews James Suzman."
3. Klein, "Ezra Klein Interviews James Suzman."

a generous providence. This is a reality reflected in the Twenty-third Psalm, where all lay down in green pastures, and it is put on display through Jesus's feeding of the five thousand who are made to sit down among the green grass in a performance of that Psalm's very hope.

On the ridge, I scan the sky. In the distance, growing closer, a Broad-winged Hawk climbs a vent of rising air. It is a pilgrim, eating from the land as it goes—a hunter with the world as its territory. I consider this bird, what it must be like to live its life—each day a reception of what the world gives. I know there are hungry days and full ones; days of effort and ease. In all of it though, it is part of the grace of the world, a grace that on this day I'd had a chance to enter. I'd seen, to paraphrase William Blake, heaven in a hawk, and entered "Eternity in an hour."

Sympathy

My younger daughter, Lucia, works a shovel beneath the surface, its blue blade pushing into the soft earth. Disturbing the layers as little as possible, she opens a space and takes the small, plastic-crated plant beside the hole. She presses on the sides of the container as I taught her to do, loosening the edges, and then slipping the plant out. Gently she places the roots in the ground, ensuring that the serrated edges of the leaves are free of loose dirt, ready to receive the sun. Without pressing too hard, she covers the roots with soil, making the gap invisible, as though this plant had grown from seed in this very place. It is fall, and we are planting strawberries for a spring harvest. When the cold comes, we'll cover the vines with deep bedding of straw and leaves, and then when the warm days of spring return we'll uncover the plants, making ready for their sweet red berries.

As I plant, I feel some strange sympathy for the strawberry vines. On an emotional, empathetic level I can sense that this is good soil and that they will be happy here. I can imagine their roots, freed of their plastic confines, joining in the community of life in this ground. I can imagine the water and sun that will help them grow. I can feel the warmth of the straw bedding, the white strands of fungi moving down into the earth, linking the strawberry roots into a sisterhood of exchange. Strange as it may seem I can imagine the life of this strawberry—what it wants, what will make it flourish, what will make it happy.

We are taught not to think this way. A plant is not animate, we're told, we shouldn't act as though it has a mind, an emotional life. The reductionist calculi of so much science tells us that to imagine a plant thinking is nothing more than anthropomorphizing.

And yet, is not this worry simply another story about the world, and an increasingly untenable one? Descartes had a story about the dogs he subjected to vivisection, nailing them to boards and cutting them open without anesthesia. As the dogs cried and yelped at the knife, Descartes dismissed the sounds as nothing more than the mechanics of their soulless bodies. We now see that as barbarous and dangerously ignorant. The medieval peasant who Descartes wanted to liberate from the confines of ignorance would have known better than to cut open a living dog without pity. She would have known, at the very least, that she was causing real suffering.

Instead of worrying about our emotional sympathy for other living things, or even the "inanimate," we should live with a humane imagination about the world. To be sympathetic is part of our gift as human beings, for it is through this imagining how other creatures live that we became human and flourished over the long run. It is dangerous when we quell that sympathetic mind for the purposes of some supposed "objectivity," a modernist fantasy of control that only covers over its own subjective agenda.

To be human is not to be one who lives by overpowering the brute realities of the world, as has been the modern mode, but is instead to tell stories about the world that deepen our sympathy with the earth and all its creatures. Indigenous wisdom can be helpful here. Robin Wall Kimmerer, a botanist and member of the Citizen Potawatomi Nation, lives on the border of the narratives of traditional wisdom and scientific rationalism. For her, science has moved in the direction of confirming much traditional wisdom rather than supplanting it with something like the Cartesian view. As Kimmerer told the journalist Krista Tippet, "I can't think of a single scientific study in the last few decades that has demonstrated that plants or animals are dumber than we think. It's always the opposite, right? What we're revealing is the fact that they have a capacity to learn, to have memory. And we're at the edge of a wonderful revolution in really understanding the sentience of other beings."[1]

To see the wisdom of a plant, to recognize its intelligence, requires an ability to read the world with attentive openness, a humble wonder. That our understanding of plants is expanding comes from just such an attentiveness. It is a new kind of science, a different kind of knowledge—one with its ear to the ground, close to the humus, sympathetic to the view of life lived from a different vantage.

1. Tippet, "Intelligence of Plants."

Reading the Ground

The other evening my family took a walk on a path near the Arkansas River. It wound along an oxbow lake, traveling through a forest of Osage Orange and Sycamores with vines creeping high into the canopy. I try to teach my daughters how to watch for tracks, and in one muddy spot we found several. There were the tracks of shoes, the waffled souls alongside the clumsy gate of domestic dogs. I could imagine a man on a jog, his labrador, ears flopping, running beside him.

Here and there, a bit older, were the hand-like prints of raccoons, their slender fingers spread into the mud. I've always found an easy kinship with raccoons. Like monkeys, there is something so like us in their hands and habits—their play, the careful washing of their food before eating. This raccoon, I imagined, was heading to the water to hunt and wash.

Beside the familiar prints, there were several I didn't at first recognize. A few inches across they were too small to be a coyote and seemed too dainty for a fox. The fingers had small nails, clearly imprinted into the mud. My first guess was river otter, an animal I've never had a clear view of in the wild, and yet from the print I could imagine the otter walking across this landscape. It was clearly good habitat. And because it had recently rained, I was pretty certain that these prints were fresh, perhaps from the night before.

In imagining an otter from the tracks on the ground, and then working from those mud-bound signs toward the wider truth of its trail—following the concrete path, wandering through the mud at the side and then slipping down into the water of the oxbow—I was forming a story in my mind of this animal and its journey. And in making that story, I was doing what every good story-teller does: I was entering the mind of the otter, trying to see the world through the otter's eyes.

Research has shown, and any reader well knows, that good stories can develop a sympathetic imagination. And this is not only true for learning to care for other human lives. Hunters, reading the story of an animal by attending to their tracks, are not only following the animal for food. In some ways, through entering the mind of the animal, they are developing sympathy for their kill. The animal and hunter have become one and the necessary pain is shared.

This truth could also be the case on a good farm. In his essay, "Why Look at Animals," John Berger wrote, "A peasant becomes fond of his pig and is glad to salt away its pork. What is significant, and is so difficult for the urban stranger to understand, is that the two statements in that sentence are connected by an *and* and not by a *but*."[1] Yet the same is not true of a thousand-hog confinement facility. Our relationship with animals has become reduced to domesticated pets, who are captive to our sameness, while moving all other animals out of our sight. We do not see the animals whose lives we destroy through the purchase of cheap furniture that takes their forests. Neither do we see or wish to understand the life of the steer that became our burger. Our sympathy for the lives from which we live has been lost and so we've become captive in an injustice.

Sympathy is critical for justice, for in its best sense, justice is an ordering of relationship; it lives in the places of concrete particularity. The hog confinement operation is able to work as it does because the individual lives of the pigs are abstracted into units. But the peasant with his pig is aware of the animal as a sentient and mortal being, like and yet unlike him. To kill the pig, he must take responsibility for it, ensuring not only that he is meeting the demands of the market but also his obligation to this animal for which he is fond. This is a reality I've experience in my own life with animals and one I see reflected in the farmers I trust to raise the meat I eat.

Justice, when operating without sympathy, becomes just another expression of Homo economicus—the mythological person who is self-interested above all else. The ancient monks of the Egyptian and Syrian deserts of the third and fourth centuries had a different conception of justice, rooted in their conception of the human person. For them, the human being was a creature, made by God and called by God to live into the light of God's grace and goodness. People were tempted toward selfishness, pride, and

1. Berger, *Selected Essays*, 261.

a host of sins that would lead to injustice, but each of these things was in fact a dehumanizing possession rather than the true reality of the person beneath. The call of discipleship, of following Christ, was to address these sins so that the full and human person beneath could emerge.

One of these desert monastics, Abba Aphrahat, the Persian Sage, wrote that "humility is the place where justice resides." The desert sages were not unlike Zen masters issuing koans, short sayings for long meditations. The Abba offered a line and then, hour upon hour, the disciple was meant to reflect on what it might mean as they wove baskets and baked bread on hot stones. In my own reflections on the statement, often in the quiet moments of walking my neighborhood, tending the soil of my garden, doing the dishes—I am struck by the idea of place in this sentence. There is a sense of grounding, the idea that humility is an address where justice dwells.

Addresses lead us to particular places, each unique—a uniform landscape of level ground and anonymous contours is always the product of violence. Real places have unique particulars—soil types, slopes, histories of life, disruptions and successions. It is humility that calls us toward those particulars, drawing us down to the ground. It is from that ground that we can do the work of justice, at least of the sort best expressed in the call of the Christian tradition. That justice is not about the following of principles, or some deontological adherence to duty. It is instead the call to love God and love neighbor, to be in right relationship with them. And that neighbor is not an abstraction for whom we organize the powers of an institution to care for and support. Instead, the justice that resides in the place of humility is a response to the one we encounter in need. It is the person we discover through the imaginative openness of sympathy through which we gather the disparate pieces of our lives and form a whole from which we are moved to act. The justice where humility dwells begins when we bend close to the ground, listening, looking, discerning the signs with sympathy for the lives who share this place with us.

The Valley of Solidarity

I work at season's end, pulling blackberry vines from around an old oak stump. They are wild and thorned, the sharp barbs penetrating even my leather work gloves. I'd let these vines grow and take over this section of my yard, spreading over the old Christmas trees I'd placed as a brush pile. A rabbit had made her nest there in the summer, the small babies venturing from its edge, ears twitching, grazing and then dashing back to the safety of the brambles. Watching for them, waiting for their small wet noses to emerge was evening entertainment for my family.

Earlier in the year in the same bramble, I was surprised to see a Mourning Warbler—grey-hooded and mustard-bodied—an elusive migrant that loves thickets. They are heard more often than seen, but this one sat up, cocking its uplifted tail like a wren. It was a win for my yard list, a bird not readily found in most urban settings.

And yet, as joyous as these encounters are, as hospitable as I try to be to the wild in my yard, I'd realized that this particular patch needed to be moved farther from the house. Creating habitat is never simple. It turns out that most of what makes a good place for birds also makes a good place for the Norway rats who end up chewing up insulation, cutting wires, and otherwise threatening the integrity of my house. Compromises must be struck, sometimes tragic truces of wild and domestic. I can see no other way, but always stay committed to the questions of where and when the compromise must be made.

As I pulled at the vines, I listened to a series of audio lectures by Thomas Merton to the novitiates at Gethsemane Abbey. Though I'd read a number of Merton's works, these lectures from a monastery classroom offered a different picture of the man. Merton's wisdom, his easy rattling off of Latin texts mixed with his jokes echoed by bursts of laughter, gave me a feeling of sitting at Merton's feet, joining with him in the life of discovering God's way.

The Valley of Solidarity

These particular lectures were about humility, following the steps of Benedict's ladder that goes down in order to go up. And in this particular session, as I pulled at the white spindles of the blackberry roots, Merton reflected on the parable in Luke's Gospel in which a banquet is held and all try to find the best seat at the table, closest to the host. The point of the parable, as Jesus explains it in one of his rare moments of didactic clarity, is to seek the lowest place, the place without honor. This, Merton taught the young men discerning their monastic vows, was the point of the life they had chosen. To be a monastic is to seek the lowest place.

Such an orientation is of course Jesus's own way in the world, one that all followers of his way should replicate in their own lives. Jesus, who could easily have sat down at the right hand of God, the place of honor, sought instead to be among the lowly. It was in seeking such a place that Christ became elevated above all.

As I listened, working in my yard, attending to the landscape, I could not help but think of how humus is always richest in the lowest places. Nutrients are always descending, death is always going down. Where that rich organic matter settles, down in the valleys, is where life flourishes. Prime agricultural land is always in the valleys, the river deltas, the places where the sediments of mountains and the flows of a thousand streams have deposited the rich material for life. And that reality of soil is a reality for human life as well.

I've lived much of my life along ridge lines and valleys, wandering up and down the slopes of Ozark mountain "hollers." As anyone who knows that landscape will tell you, the trees in the valley are taller than those on the hills. On the slope of the mountain where I farmed, there was a stand of ancient oaks that a botanist friend once suggested were old growth, never cut in the logging operations that cleared most of the mountain—and yet they were thin and short compared to the younger trees in the valley below. Wind and lack of water had shaped them for the heights, and what survives at the top never grows tall.

I remember as a child, wandering the fields and forests near my home and finding a hollow with a waterfall, deep in the woods. Standing on its edge, I was struck by the height of the white oaks whose lower canopies were at eye level as I stood on the ridge above. They had grown straight and tall, reaching for the sun, nourished by the creek that cut the valley through the layers of sandstone and shale. Their crowns were nearly on par with the trees on the hillsides and yet they were several meters taller from ground to peak.

I've never been to the deserts of Egypt, the wadis of Syria, but I imagine that trees follow a similar pattern of growth—the canyons and settled places of the river beds, yielding the most height. It was in those landscapes that Iperechious, a fifth-century abba of the desert, lived. He taught that "Humility makes the tree of life grow to its highest."[1] If we are to grow to the heights, the consistent wisdom is that we should go to the valleys.

My back bent, my hands stinging, I felt the downward pull of my body. "Justice is the place where humility resides," the journey has been to find that location. Merton following Benedict following Jesus says that it is the lowest place at the table, the place without honor. Iperechious says that it is in the valley, the place from which the tree of life can grow its highest.

Where is justice here? Where is humility? I look around my backyard. There is too much clay, humus is hard to find. There are patches of weeds, everywhere, signaling the soil's deficiencies. Justice has not arrived here, right relationship has not found its harmony. But it is starting. I can look across the landscape and begin to imagine what might come. There are dozens of trees that weren't here when we started. My compost piles are drawing in the life that sparks the cascades of flourishing. Each day we capture waste and turn it toward decay, returning it to the soil.

What would it mean to live justly here? It's a question always on my mind. But perhaps my mind has little to offer in answering it. Maybe I need to pay more attention to my body, the places where beauty springs forth. Jesus is the righteousness of God, or so says the Christian story after all. Jesus is the Word made flesh. Jesus is the God who became animal. Maybe the way toward justice is to follow that path, living in obedience to the animals we were made to be.

And maybe in becoming animal, we can find a way into the compromises of justice that cling to any serious attending—the finite struggles that always follow us as we seek to live rightly. How can I be responsible to the multitude of creatures that share this place with me and show them hospitality while also preserving the integrity of my home? How can I be hospitable to neighbors or the poor, when there are often intractable questions that get in the way? It's a question of justice that God engaged with the oddest compromise of all—the Word become flesh, the Incarnation of God into a human.

---

1. Louf, *Way of Humility*, 37.

Even on the Hilltops

In the winter months, when sitting on the porch is too cold, Emily and I have our coffee by a window looking out at the backyard. We face east, watching the rising sun and welcoming the morning birds that begin to move among the trees. Eventually, our daughters wake, sleepily entering the room. At the end of our conversation, Emily and I read the morning Psalm, the one appointed in *The Book of Common Prayer* for that day. The girls are invited to join us, and often they want to, taking a rotation in our responsive reading.

Recently the morning selection was Psalm 72. It is a royal song, one calling for a king who lives fully into the ways of God, a vision for the eventual messiah. "Give the king your justice, O God," it begins. The king needs God's justice, not for raw power, but so that he might reflect that justice in his rule of the land: "That he may rule your people righteously and the poor with justice . . . He shall defend the needy among the people; he shall rescue the poor and crush the oppressor."

At the end of the Psalm, there is an image rooted in soil ecology: "May there be an abundance of grain on the earth," sings the psalmist, "growing thick even on the hilltops." For grain to grow thick on the hilltops means that the soil there must be rich and fertile, not eroded down to the valleys. As any agricultural society would know, such a reality is rare, especially in tilled fields where the soil is disrupted.

As we finished the Psalm, I looked out at the backyard. Rains had come recently, washing away some of the mulch I'd put in place. I was reminded of the need to build new swales, beginning at the top of the slope and moving down from there. These combinations of a ditch and mound, running along the contour, help hold the water, slowing its flow and pushing it down into the earth. Swales also help build and keep soil, slowing the loss of organic matter.

Having read Psalm 72, thinking of my swales, I wondered about the grain on the hilltops. To have grain on the hilltops, one would need something like swales, a way to slow the flow of water and keep the soil in place. Included could be strips of permanent ground cover, like the prairie strips pioneered by the ecologist Lisa Schulte Moore in the Midwest—belts of native, perennial plants that help slow the rate of soil erosion and provide habitat for a variety of creatures.[1] To make soil rich, even on the hilltops, is to make the heights like the valleys.

Grain on the hilltops is a metaphor of the kind of abundance that a just king will bring, but such justice is clearly echoed in the ecological realities of Israel. Chaos in creation reflects an economy of abuse, a politics of exploitation. To have health in all the aspects of the land is a reality that can only happen when even the soil is cared for in the Great Economy of God. The political implications of this care for the soil are many, but at its heart is a kind of flourishing on every level. Rather than the heights relying on the exploitation of the valleys, the hilltops and the valleys should be joined in a shared abundance of good soil.

"Solidarity is the social meaning of humility," writes the Jesuit Dean Brackley.[2] It is solidarity with the poor, with the lowly, that brings the common flourishing of creation, from hilltop to valley. Such solidarity is the model of the messianic king—the model that Jesus fulfilled with perfection. His was in every way a journey to the valleys, a journey of solidarity with all the lowly. And yet it was there that the good soil of flourishing could be found. And now that Jesus has ascended to the heights, seated at the right hand of God—that humility continues.

What if we demanded such a pattern from our leaders, the highest places and offices reflecting the valleys where good soil lies? What should be put in place, what swales and prairie strips are necessary, to make the hilltops like the valleys so that grain might grow abundantly and even those in the high places contribute to our common flourishing?

These are the kinds of questions of our common life that a text like Psalm 72 demands. We find the answers in the life of Jesus, the king who lived like the lowly, who accepted humiliation and humility rather than power. It was in that act that Jesus became king above all, the highest places and the lowest places, all joined in the common goodness of his kingdom.

---

1. See MacArthur Foundation website, https://www.macfound.org/fellows/class-of-2021/lisa-schulte-moore.

2. Quoted in O'Brien, *Ignatian Adventure*, 174.

Pruning to Pattern

One Easter morning a few years back, my daughters woke to find that the Easter Bunny had not brought them a load of tasteless marshmallows, cheap chocolate rabbits, and consumerist crap (crap, actually, would have been fine, as long as it was good for compost). The Easter Bunny had, instead, brought them a couple of trees along with a handful of quality chocolate truffles. They didn't stop to question the discrepancy between their gifts and those received by neighbors. Instead, they seemed honestly excited about the trees and the fruit they would bare. We planted them in the ground soon after Easter.

Only one survived the summer, and now, several years later, this pear tree is over 20 feet high. It sits in a swale on the south side of our front yard, next to a yaupon holly, an American Beautyberry, and a button bush. Around the base we planted comfrey, an herbal plant good for cuts and stings that is regarded as an aid to compost and a helpful companion to fruit trees. It's a perennial with roots that go deep, drawing up the nutrients from below.

Last summer, with good rains early in the season and a mild start to the summer, the pear flowered well and was soon laden with fruit. Too laden, in fact, because the branches in some of the upper parts of the tree began to snap and break under their weight. The lower branches became intertwined, creating a nice ladder for the resident rats and squirrels to climb and wipe out most of the fruit. It was not a good year, and I felt a failure. But like most gardeners with a bad year, I had the next season, always another chance to get it right.

In the new year, as winter was waning, but spring had not yet come, I set out to prune the pear tree. I have little experience with pruning and so I turned to the how-to source most of us do these days: YouTube. There were, of course, a wide variety of results of varying credibility, but I chose to watch one video by an older man who carried the authority of experience, starting with the need for the right tools and the proper way to sharpen them (always a good sign).

Demonstrating on a young tree, he talked through the logic of pruning and how to determine what to cut. The goal is to make the harvest easier, reduce the burden of fruit on the branches, and reduce diseases and pests. After I felt like I had a good sense of how to do it all, I went out one sunny day with a saw and sharp shears, and began the work of pruning. I couldn't help but think, as I was doing so, of Masanobu Fukuoka.

Fukuoka was a pioneer of the "natural farming" movement. His book, *The One-straw Revolution*, now published in the New York Review of Books Classics series, reflects its stature. The book follows Fukuoka's journey as a young farmer attempting to grow food by letting nature be—the quiet way of releasing control. One of his early lessons was with pruning.

Fukuoka inherited a citrus orchard from his father. He decided to use the orchard as a place where he could experiment with his philosophy of "do-nothing farming." His aim was a kind of restful agriculture, guided not by the question of what can I do, but what can be left undone. Fukuoka said he was always asking, "How about *not* doing this? How about *not* doing that?" Which led him to ask, how about not pruning the citrus orchard?

The results were not good, initially. Fukuoka lost almost two acres of mandarin orange trees due to insects and disease. It took the loss of another 400 trees before he felt like he had trees surviving in what he could say was "the natural pattern."[1]

What Fukuoka came to see is that farming according to nature's way was difficult in systems that already had strayed away from it. "To the extent that trees deviate from their natural form," he wrote, "pruning and insect extermination become necessary."[2] Pruning is required because the natural systems of control have been disrupted. Farming, cultivation, domestication—these are disruptions of the natural form. How do we then deal with the consequences of agriculture in a way that conforms more closely to nature's pattern?

I bought my pear tree before reading Fukuoka. It was a domestic variety that had already been pruned. The die had been cast and now it was dependent on me, or at least so I felt. It's a problem with which Fukuoka was well aware. "Most seedling trees have been pruned or their roots have

---

1. Fukuoka, *One-straw Revolution*, 15.
2. Fukuoka, *One-straw Revolution*, 15.

Pruning to Pattern

been damaged at the nursery before they are transplanted to the orchard, which makes pruning necessary right from the start," he writes. The path of natural farming becomes, then, not a path of abandonment (as he experimented with early in his work) but of patient rehabilitation: " . . . if trees are gradually corrected, they will return at least approximately to their natural form. The trees become stronger and measures to control insects become unnecessary."[3]

In this pattern, the goal of pruning should be to not prune. This is a pattern of humble justice; it is the way of *metanoia*—a change of life. It does not mean inaction—a total passivity. Instead, the call is a careful watching and tending of the whole, a reality we can never completely understand.

There's a curious coda to Fukuoka's decision to abandon pruning his citrus trees. He writes that instead of pruning, he introduced a Morishima acacia tree that flowers and fruits in all seasons. In some permaculture circles the tree is called a "fertilizer tree" because it fixes nitrogen in the soil, helping feed the surrounding trees and plants. Fukuoka's acacia attracted aphids in large numbers and those aphids then attracted lady bugs. When the lady bugs ate all the aphids, they then began to feed on the pests on other nearby trees, including the mandarins.

On the surface, this looks like a story of nature working, the systems of life taking care of themselves. But there is a catch. The acacia Fukuoka planted is native to Australia not Japan. It was imported to Japan for the purposes of agriculture and ornament. To introduce is it into his ecological system was then no act of pristine ecology, a natural system left all to its own. And perhaps that is also part of the point, too. We are tenders, adapters, and controllers of the world. We cannot just let things be nor should we.

What we must resist is the pattern of Cain, the impulse to control without keeping, to work without preservation. How to bring these two realities together in the world we have so altered and changed is a question we must continually be asking—it is one I now ask every year when the time comes to prune.

---

3. Fukuoka, *One-straw Revolution*, 60.

The Obedience of Trees

In the late winter, just before the earth's final tilt toward the sun, I moved a tree. It was small, six feet at most—a magnolia planted as a sapling a few years before. The placement, we thought, would be a good one. Plenty of sunlight and good drainage, and the tree would act as a screen from the intersection behind us.

The earth, however, had other plans. Shortly after planting the magnolia, a hackberry began to grow nearby—in a couple of years it was over twenty feet tall. These are trees that many people consider "junk" trees— early succession plants that aren't of much value for timber or ornament. But they are ecological gold, the food host for the caterpillars of tawny emperor, hackberry emperor, mourning cloak, question mark, and American snout butterflies. Those caterpillars are then food for birds from warblers to chickadees. In the fall and winter, the tree's berries are a ready source of nutrients for cedar waxwings and robins, birds that spread the seeds in their waste, planting more trees as they go. Given all of that ecological richness, I didn't want to cut a hackberry that had freely grown in my yard, so I opted to move the magnolia instead.

My daughter wanted to help, so together we began to cut around the base of the tree with our shovels, mine long handled, a grey-brown of worn metal; hers a red-bladed shovel just right for her height. We tried to keep as much of the main root ball intact as we cut, working down around the base until the tree began to shift sideways, ready to be pulled up.

We'd prepared a new hole for the tree in a good sunny spot a bit farther from the house. As a welcome, we'd put some of my best compost at the bottom of the hole. Once we had lowered the root ball in, filling the dirt around, we tamped it into place with our boots. I then took some partially composted mulch from the nearby pile, stringy with the white fibers of fungi, and spread it thickly around the base. The mulch, if it worked, would

The Obedience of Trees

help establish a healthy mycorrhizal community for the tree—connecting it to the nutrients of the soil and the other plants in this new place.

I hope that this tree, planted here on the edge of my yard, roots drawn out in the muddy soil, will one day be a prayer—an act of glorifying God its creator. "This particular tree will give glory to God by spreading out its roots in the earth and raising its branches into the air and the light in a way that no other tree before or after it ever did or will do," Thomas Merton once wrote of another sylvan saint.[1] In doing this the tree is being obedient to God, for it is enacting what God made it to be.

Obedience is a common theme in the literature on humility. St. Bernard of Clairvaux, following in the footsteps of St. Benedict, puts obedience at the center of steps 2-4 of his ascending ladder of humility: "Not to love one's own will . . . To submit to superiors in obedience . . . To hold fast to patience amidst hard and rough things for the sake of obedience."[2] One can imagine the value of these principles in the life of a monastery, but why are they so central to the way of humility? Do we really have to be obedient in order to be humble?

Over the last several centuries, our vision of a flourishing life has been uncoupled from obedience. Language like that of St. Bernard's is viewed with suspicion, read as a guise by which the powerful have subjected the scrupulous. And so, in the name of liberation, we reject all forms of obedience—to God, our givenness, or one another.

And yet, the New Testament and early centuries of Christianity show a different way, one that should call us to restore rather than reject obedience. As St. Paul so clearly saw it, we are slaves whether we like it or not—our desires are captive to sin. What if, paradoxically, the way to actual rather than formal freedom is the way of obedience to the one who can make us free?

Our problem goes back to Adam, which is to say the roots of who we are as human beings. Adam, as the archetypal first human, was given life. With that life, quite apart from anything the *adam* did or chose, was both a value and a vocation. In Genesis 1, the creation of human beings was judged to

1. Merton, *New Seeds*, 29.
2. Bernard, *Steps of Humility and Pride*, 27.

be "very good," and in Genesis 2 the humus-being was placed in the garden to "serve and preserve it." The work, then, of human life was to be obedient to that givenness—to express that value and vocation.

In the deep wisdom of the story, however, we find the human problem. The first temptation was to be more than human. As Johannes Baptist Metz puts it, "Satan always tries to stress the spiritual strength of human beings and our divine character . . . 'You will be like God': that is Satan's slogan. It is *the* temptation the Evil One has set before us in countless variations, urging us to reject the truth about the humanity we have been given."[3] The disobedience of the first humans, then, was not a violation of some abstract rule, but was instead a rebellion against their givenness—a desire to be something other than human. The dangerous thing about Jesus was that he was willing to be human, to really be human in all the fragility and poverty that this creaturely life entails.

This willingness to live into creaturely life is put on display when Jesus is tempted in the wilderness with "strength, security, and spiritual abundance"(see Matt 4:1–11).[4] In obedience to God, Jesus willingly enters into the poverty of human life rather than alleviating his condition. "For hunger becomes a human hunger only when it can never be fully allayed," writes Metz, "desire becomes a human desire only when it can remain unfulfilled. And nearness to the abyss becomes a human experience only when one can no longer call upon helping hands for protection."[5] Christ experienced all of these things, and as such he became fully human.

Most of us avoid becoming fully human. We don't want to accept the basic lack and dependence, the essential poverty and vulnerability of human life. Rather than being creatures from the soil, dependent upon it, we want to control earth and even escape it. Sin, as Metz points out, "does not heighten the saga or the suffering of our uncertain plight; instead, it compromises and mitigates them. Enmeshed in sin, we do not drink in our poverty down to the last drop; we do not stare it full in the face."[6] This essential poverty of our nature, the vulnerability that Karl Barth called the shadow side of creation, is not the result of sin but is instead what drives us to it. We make an alliance with the Nothing, the true Death of annihilation, in order to escape being fully human. It was Christ who refused the

---

3. Metz, *Poverty of Spirit*, 11.
4. Metz, *Poverty of Spirit*, 11.
5. Metz, *Poverty of Spirit*, 11.
6. Metz, *Poverty of Spirit*, 12–13.

deal with the devil, the alleviation of human creatureliness, who was able to finally recover the fullness of human life. In his humility he set out a pattern of what it means to be human once again.

Thomas Merton, reflecting on the obedience of a tree, wrote that "a tree imitates God by being a tree . . . The more a tree is like itself, the more it is like Him."[7] Our problem is that we do not live into our lives as human beings. Instead, we seek to be something more and other, to transcend our limits. So it is that we put on masks, creating selves that cover over our forgetting. The journey of human obedience is, in a way, the reverse of a tree's. For us, the more we are like him, that is Jesus, the more we are ourselves.

Paul works out this reality in chapter 5 of his letter to the Roman church. There Paul is working to name our situation and what Christ did to change it. Christ, he says, is the new *adam*—the new ancestor and model for what human life might be. "Many people were made righteous through the obedience of one person, just as many people were made sinners through the disobedience of one person" (Rom 5:19 CEB). Interestingly, the Greek word used for obedience here is also the term for attentiveness, for listening. The obedience that means our salvation and liberation is one that is based not in blind submission, but in attentive listening to the Word that is our source. It was Jesus who attended to that word, who lived it so fully that he was that Word. He listened to the song of life, the given song to which we are all called to join. In that listening he was able to return humanity to its true self—to sing the part given to us in the polyphony of creation. We speak of the Incarnation as God becoming human, of Christ taking on flesh. What Christ did, in this movement, was also to create a path for our own incarnation—a way for all of the children of Adam to remember how to be human.

To listen to the soil, to train our ear to the sound of trees, this is an attending by which we can begin to hear the hum of our human chorus in the song of all creation. Like Jesus whose temptation came after forty days of listening to trees and wind and rock in the wilderness, we can begin to recover our own creaturely nature in such silence, especially silence in the given world of God's grace. It is a way of hearing by which we can rest in our vulnerability before God, hearing the whispered song of creation covered

7. Merton, *New Seeds*, 29.

over by our constant noise. When we begin to practice what theologian Sarah Coakley calls a "defenseless prayer of silent waiting on God" we can move into a greater obedience, an obedience like a tree.[8]

8. Coakley, *Powers and Submissions*, 34.

Theosis

The spring rains have turned toward summer, everything bursting with life, the ground smelling of its hunger and rot, life everywhere eating and being eaten in a lush frenzy. On my hikes through the forest park near my home, in washed out places where the water descends down hillsides, pushing the leaves to the sides of small gullies, the orange trumpet-shaped chanterelles fruit in the curtain of humid air. Sometimes, I catch their scent, a sweet and inviting hint of their flavor.

Last night, after a day of rain, the storm mostly moved on, a group of us gathered in the woods for our usual worship among the trees. The rain had cooled the air and turned the scent of the ground fresh. The Gospel reading for the day was from John 17, a portion of the longest prayer of Jesus recorded in the Scriptures. It is a prayer of blessing and petition for his disciples on the eve of his arrest. The prayer is beautiful and mystical and at its heart is an idea that is deeply radical—that his disciples might join in God's own life.

"Father, just as you are in me and I am in you, I pray that they also will be in us" (John 17:21). There is no sermon at this service. Instead we hear the Gospel and walk out into the woods, wandering and watching, looking for anything that might catch our attention and offer us insight.

Not far from the small pile of stones that forms our altar, some chanterelles were growing in a washed out spot on the hillside. I cut the largest one at the stem, smelling its delicate aroma before setting it down on the shale slab. This mushroom, the fruit of a life that lives and moves and connects beneath the surface, was as good a metaphor I could imagine of what Jesus was praying for. It is a symbol of coming together into a deep and profound union.

At the end of the world, there is God and there is creation. But this end is not a circle returned to its start. Creation has become something new, creation has become part of God. A membership within the divine life.

When a forest begins again after a fire or a cut, it begins a process of succession. In the early stages all is raucous with life, a carnival of individuals all seeking to survive. But as the forest matures, the individual elements of its life begin to settle into a wholeness. With time, in the slow language of the soil, trees become connected to one another, species begin to cooperate, life settles into a rhythm in which each member joins the common dance. There is still room made for newness, old trees die and give way to new ones, animals are born and return to the earth, but in each stage and moment here is a unity that has been reached. We can speak of each species, each individual, but it becomes harder the more developed the ecosystem to fully separate them.

Creation, in a way, is moving toward this common dance on a cosmic scale. It is a reality known in theology as theosis, the way in which the creature, especially the human creature, becomes enclosed in God—sharing in some mysterious way in God's life and fullness. Theosis is a becoming, but it does not mean that we arrive at some independent status of divinity or that we lose our creaturely existence, free of finitude. It means instead that we have settled into a wholeness, that we have become, in some mysterious way, a part of the God who was and is and will ever be. And how do we join in God, our lives becoming divine? It is the path of humility—the going down to the ground of all things. It is there that we encounter the very heart of God's personhood.

That Jesus prayed for his disciples to be united with God on the eve of his crucifixion is no accident. It was his self-offering, his kenotic act of obedience that carried him toward the cross. It was the cross that opened the way for his followers to join in the God-life through their own self-giving. As theologian Andrew Root puts it, theosis "is to be drawn in to the being of God through the humility of the kenotic. Theosis is the ontological transformation of sharing in the being of God by encountering the kenotic energy of God, which seeks to share in hypostasis or personhood through the experience of death (the cross)."[1] Root speaks here in the technical language of theology, so let me try to put it in plainer terms, a bit closer to the ground.

---

1. Root, *Faith Formation in a Secular Age*, 178.

THEOSIS

God's nature is that of giver, continually offering himself to the world. To be joined into the life and reality of God is to also live a life of offering, a self-giving rooted in humility. When we do this there is a way in which our very being is transformed, joined into God's own reality and personhood. We have ceased to be merely our own selves, focused on our own ends, but have instead entered the entangled living whole of God. Our lives have joined into the song of all creation, the pattern of God's personhood that echoes through all things. It is when we offer ourselves for the sake of the other that our lives reflect the "kenotic energy of God," our lives humming along in the same tune as God's life. Theosis is not about becoming God with all of the attributes of God, achieving omniscience and omnipotence and all of those "transcendentals" we attribute to the Divine. Instead, in theosis, we reflect God's personhood to such a degree that our lives become connected and related to God's life—a wholeness of settled solidarity.

At home, later that week I pour a wheelbarrow of compost across a garden bed. It is dark like chocolate, the smell sweet—filaments of fungi clinging to clumps of soil here and there. This humus began from death— limbs cut from trees, grass cut for straw, vegetables trimmed. But now, it is something new, it is joined and connected to a whole, made alive with breath. What turns rot and decay into new and life-giving soil is breath, the aerobic processes of microbes. And so it is with us, the breath of God entering the dead and dying world, and turning it red like a fire fueled by oxygen, red like blood blooming with a gasp. God's spirit has been poured into our hearts and with that breath we are being joined into something new—our lives no longer lost in our aloneness but shared in the very being of the God who has always been our source.

Paradise Lot

At night we hear gunshots, blasts echoing across the concrete canyon of the interstate. That road, six lanes and growing, divided the city, south and north, black and white, poor and better off. We live on the edge, a remnant neighborhood of what was once more common—a community of varied races and incomes. South, however, the pressures of poverty and addiction reign and guns are all too easy to get. So we hear the pop, pop, pop of a semiautomatic and read the newspaper reports about the latest murders.

During the day, there are the wandering ranters, talking to the ghosts that haunt them, yelling with an inarticulate rage at the source of their broken minds. I know we are supposed to speak in terms of mental health and brain chemistry, but what I see feels more like possession than a disease. The white plastic bracelets on the wrists of so many who walk through my neighborhood bear witness to the failure of medicine against so unmovable a mountain.

And all of this happens under the constant whir of tires, the traffic running past on the anonymous roads, carrying people locked in steel boxes through the nowhere of the in-betweens of where they are and where they want to be. I know the way, because I often travel those same roads.

Sometimes my wife and I catch each other sitting before the glow of the computer screen, real estate listings pulled up, longing for someplace else. Maybe we'll move to the country some day where we can have some acreage, animals, a bit quieter life. But what are we to make of our life now? Are we in a purgatory between heaven in the country and the hell of urban life? Heaven as an elsewhere has a long tradition, but hell has always seemed closer at hand.

It is mid-winter, the edges of night expanding from either edge of day—the dark's blanket covering the earth for longer sleep. The White-throated Sparrows, arrived from their boreal summers, work the fallen leaves for a scrap of seed. All flowers have now faded, with even the Prairie Fleabane gone to seed.

The winter may seem an odd season to favor, but I have always loved it. Winters here are mild, with snaps of cold punctuating weather that is mostly comfortable with only a sweater. It is in the winter that birds flock to the state, and wandering species thrill local birders with their rare appearances. It is in the winter that last year's mistakes in the garden are undone and a new season can be readied for without the constant flush of life to keep up with.

I go to the public library downtown, not far from the church. It is the de facto day center for many who are homeless, the victims of trauma and addiction, those caught in the hell of a broken society. I'm here to check out a book I've read before, one of my first introductions to the practice of permaculture: *Paradise Lot*.

It is the story of how Eric Toensmeier and Jonathan Bates, two self-proclaimed "plant geeks," moved to a duplex in urban Holyoke, Massachusetts. The yard, front and back, made up a tenth of an acre—not much by any agricultural standard. It was not a particularly promising place—just an urban yard not much different from mine. But with work, skill, and know-how, Toensemeier and Bates transformed the yard into an urban oasis of edible landscaping—a paradise in the middle of a broken city.

Flipping through the pictures in the book that chronicle the yard's transformation, I see a yard of patchy grass, overshadowed by a neighbor's maple. Then there are the pictures of the gardening work that transformed the ground, followed by the young plants they nestled throughout the space. Finally, there are the images of the mature landscape—a place from which they can gather food any month of the year, a space that provides habitat and food and beauty to a wide variety of neighbors, domestic and wild.

What Toensmeier and Bates create—or better, welcomed into their yard—is what I want to welcome into this place. It is what I want to be able to invite to any place I occupy for any length of time—paradise arriving on abused and broken ground. The work began for them, it should be no surprise, with the soil. They used a sheet mulching technique on the whole yard—layering mineral amendments, compost, cardboard, more compost, straw and wood chips until everything was covered in a thick layer of biologically enriched organic matter. It was from this ground that their paradise began. And it is from the ground that any hope of paradise must spring.

⁂

Paradise in the Bible is a complex reality, one whose nuances are not fully understood, and we could spend volumes exploring. But from Isaiah to Revelation there is the image of all creation renewed, everything participating in the heavenly reality. And in the end, like the Incarnation itself, God comes down—heaven comes to earth so that paradise is not some elsewhere but is present here, in the nearby places of our neighborhoods.

That is the *eschaton*, the last and final place, that is the end toward which all things reach and aim. And just as Jesus is the first fruit of this new reality, the early harvest after the frost, this final age is already showing up in the world of the here and now. It appears especially among those who have chosen to be last, so that they may be the first to enter this age of all last things. These are the ones who have taken on the humble path of Christ and so can live in the expectation that they will live into the resurrection reality Christ has already come to occupy.

In John's Gospel, in one of his first encounters after being raised from the dead, Jesus meets Mary Magdalene in the garden. She is upset, having found the tomb empty. Jesus comes to her, but she doesn't recognize him, mistaking him for the gardener. It is a case of mistaken identity pregnant with symbol and meaning. In seeing the resurrected Christ as a gardener, she is recognizing something of Jesus's new reality—he is the human alive fully again and as such he embodies the human vocation to serve and preserve the creation.

In Jesus, we find the fulfillment of the vocation that Adam, the first humus-being, did not—Jesus is the gardener of a new Eden, cultivating a paradise restored. Now we who follow Jesus should also become gardeners, learning to "practice resurrection." As the biblical scholar William P. Brown puts it, "Gardeners are, in fact, practitioners of resurrection, of bringing forth new life from below, from out of the rich, decaying, organic soil. The human from the humus." What gardeners enact on a small, limited scale, reflecting the image of God, is what God enacts on a cosmic scale. As Brown goes on to say:

> Resurrection includes the whole of life in its vast eschatological and ecological sweep, all from the simple fact that we remain, now

and forevermore, tied to God's creation . . . Resurrection is hands down the most miraculous act of cultivation, and it is also the most essential act of cultivation: the eruption of new life out of the soil that is our flesh. Resurrection is God's cosmic victory garden.[1]

We who now live in the shadow of that resurrection are called to live in the possibility of a renewed humanity. And as such, we are invited into that same work, imitating Christ in renewing the work that Adam was called to do. We too are called to become human beings fully alive, humans who live into our vocation of serving and preserving a creation that voices its praise to God. It is a work, if we learn to live into it, that we could do forever and it begins by cultivating paradise now, as an act of hope in the future God is bringing.

---

1. Brown, *Sacred Sense*, 135–36.

Forever Work

Yesterday, I worked at weeding some Bermuda grass that had taken root around my perennial herbs. The day was unseasonably warm, and the air carried with it a hint of coming rain. I usually prefer to work closer to the ground, but the weeds demanded that I begin with a larger tool—a long-handled hoe. There are a variety of hoes, each shaped differently for the work at hand. This one was made for more detailed work, narrow enough to remove weeds without upsetting the soil too much. Some call it an onion hoe for its ability to work around root vegetables without destroying the crop.

I'm not sure where I acquired my onion hoe, but as I worked with it, I appreciated its craftsmanship. The tool seemed sturdier and better built than many of the cheap ones on sale at the average big box hardware store. Its shape and build reflected someone who knows what it means to work with a tool like this rather than someone intent only on selling one.

When I'd made a few passes with the hoe, I followed up with the hori hori, pulling out the white rhizomes that clung to the clay beneath. And though I'd like to imagine that paradise will be free of weeds like Bermuda grass, there was a moment doing this work when I felt like it was something I could go on doing forever—that this work was not in conflict with rest, that it could continue into an eternity because it conforms in some deep way to the self-renewing life of creation.

What projects, what work could we continue into the full coming of God's reign? What things *must* cease in that coming? What things *will* cease and what will continue? These are important questions and in working through them we can find helpful guidance for our living now.

Forever Work

For Toensemeier and Bates, their creation of a "paradise lot," was the formation of a space that occupied more and more of the future in its fullness. They took an ecological desert and turned it toward an oasis of life. It is not complete or perfect, but its life is being moved toward the future—not a future of disruption and upheaval, though their garden could be a refuge in such time—but more so for a future of restoration and renewal.

Paradise is not here, yet, but it is beginning. The goal should be to welcome it, making our lives congruent with its coming. Our hope should not be a disruption that undoes everything in our lives and rearranges them, but rather a consummation of what has already begun. The work of change, of repentance in its truest sense, is to live with congruence toward God's future.

We can find some help in imagining this from what's called the Transition movement. As one of its documents defines it, "Transition is an ongoing social experiment, a movement of communities coming together to reimagine and rebuild our world through a process of creating healthy human culture."[1] The aim is to help communities move into a flourishing future for humankind and the planet, living now into the reality to which they hope to transition.

This is not a bad description of what the church is called toward. We are to be communities of transition from the chaos and disease of a life out of balance, a life tempted toward Nothingness. The church is a place where we learn and practice, in the midst of the world as it now is, the realities of the flourishing future that is coming. It is a community of congruence with creation, ready to end creation's groaning by offering moments of assuagement until God brings the final peace.

That idea of creation waiting in groaning comes from Paul's letter to the church in Rome, the magnum opus of the great apostle. Late in that letter, Paul offers a vision of the church as a transition movement toward God's reign. In what we now call the Romans 13, Paul reminds the church that they "know what time it is." The word he uses here is *kairos*—the season of God's arrival. As Paul puts it, "the night is far gone, the day is near." When we realize this, when we realize that we are not locked into the inevitabilities of the world as it is, then we can begin living into a different future. It is a future we start to inhabit, Paul tells us, by "putting on Christ." We enter the world of paradise by taking on the humble clothes of Jesus's way.

---

1. Transition Network Team, *Essential Guide*.

RETURN

My wife texts me as I prepare to lead a Eucharist. It is a Tuesday, an election day in November. Anxiety is again high as it now always seems to be on such days. My church has chosen to worship God rather than enter the frantic waiting for the polls to close. Our concern is not who will win congress, who will be our next governor. Those are not bad concerns, but they are not the determining factors of our hope. It was fitting then that Emily wrote to remind me to order trees. We're continuing our work to provide more habitat in our yard, to rewild it, or as the landscape designer Benjamin Voigt prefers to put it, we're seeking to practice reconciliation ecology.

Our trees won't be ready until the mid-winter, when all seems dead and dormant, but it is then that trees are best established. As the local nursery website puts, mid-winter is "tree planting season." A *kairos* time in what Christina Rosetti so beautifully named the "bleak midwinter."

> Our God, Heaven cannot hold Him, nor earth sustain;
> Heaven and earth shall flee away when He comes to reign.
> In the bleak midwinter a stable place sufficed
> The Lord God Almighty, Jesus Christ.[2]

To plant trees, pressing into the wet clay of the saturated earth of the winter ground, is an act of welcoming the season of Incarnation, a renewal made possible by small things. As Rosetti expresses it, the God who is beyond all was satisfied to dwell in the particular of a place, to be born in a stable. And in that Incarnation Christ established a new reality, a season of new life that was seeded even in the midwinter, planting for the renewal of all things.

In Romans 13, Paul is telling us that the situation of the church is in the midwinter. The days have become as short as they will grow, the cold as bitter as it will get. Now is the time to plant trees, to spread the life now dormant that will grow into the abundance of a garden, a paradise soon enough.

Such a paradise is not a future we make, but instead is a future we join, a future we are claimed by in Christ. That is the difference between Christian faith and both progressive politics and conservative return. Progress for whom, progress in what? Return to what? The coming of God's kingdom is the healing of all things; it is the final justice of the world and

---

2. From "In the Bleak Midwinter" by Christina Rosetti.

Forever Work

it is already arriving outside of both the future and the past. Our work is to join in that arrival, to hear its song even when the tune is hard to follow amid the clanging noise of the machine world.

To plant trees is to enter a harmony, a congruence with the future that God is bringing, especially when those trees are species that will serve the diverse life of this particular place. The Incarnation is always particular; it is the invitation to the healing of each place according to its own needs. And this, I think, is true of the coming of God into the world once again.

Congruence with the kingdom is a key task of the creaturely life made whole, and it is something we can move into with greater and greater ease and fullness. Growing up, I never learned a musical instrument. It wasn't until seminary that I even vaguely began to understand how to read music. But my daughters are both learning instruments and how to decipher the strange notations of sound. They can sit down with sheet music before them and turn the signs and symbols into beautiful sound. And as they get better, as their playing improves and their skills increase, I know that they will be able to play with ever greater clarity and fullness and complexity. They will add, eventually, their own style to the competent execution of the notes.

I think it is the same with our work toward God's paradise. We learn the music, how to read it, and we begin to play, fitfully at first and then with growing competence we get the notes right in ever more complex arrangements. But when we finally hit our stride, when our skills are more fully developed, we can bring into the music our own style, our own personhood. Style is a natural outgrowth of our work and it is part of God's way of inviting the complex and varied expressions of creation. Industry seeks uniformity, but creation always bends toward unique renditions of our common song.

The music of creation is already humming in the humus; it is already echoing across the land. The work I am called to, the work we all are called to, is to listen to that music, to lift our voices and pick up our instruments, to join in the song with our voice and style that is like no other. When that music has reached its fullness, every voice joined in its unique and full expression, then we will have arrived at paradise.

Bibliography

Anderson, M. Kat. *Tending the Wild: Native American Knowledge and the Management of California's Natural Resources*. Berkeley, CA: University of California Press, 2005.
Anonymous. *The Cloud of Unknowing and Other Works*. Translated by A. C. Spearing. New York: Penguin, 2001.
Arendt, Hannah. *Eichmann in Jerusalem: A Report on the Banality of Evil*. New York: Penguin, 2006.
Becker, Ernst. *The Denial of Death*. New York: Free Press, 1997.
Berger, John. *Selected Essays*. Edited by Geoff Dyer. New York: Vintage, 2001.
Berry, Wendell. *What Are People For?* New York: North Point, 1990.
Bradatan, Costica. "In Praise of Failure." *New York Times*, December 15, 2013. https://archive.nytimes.com/opinionator.blogs.nytimes.com/2013/12/15/in-praise-of-failure/.
Brown, William P. *Sacred Sense: Discovering the Wonder of God's Word and World*. Grand Rapids: Eerdmans, 2015.
Bulgakov, Sergius. *The Holy Grail and the Eucharist*. Trans. Boris Jakim. Hudson, NY: Lindisfarne, 1997.
Casey, Michael. *A Guide to Living in the Truth: Saint Benedict's Teaching on Humility*. Ligouri, MO: Liguori, 2001.
Chapman, John. *Spiritual Letters*. Repr. New York: Burns & Oates, 2004.
Coakley, Sarah. *Powers and Submissions: Spirituality, Philosophy and Gender*. Malden, MA: Blackwell, 2002.
Crawford, Matthew. *The World Beyond Your Head: Becoming an Individual in an Age of Distraction*. New York: Penguin, 2015.
Delio, Ilia, OSF. *The Humility of God: A Franciscan Perspective*. Cincinnati: Franciscan Media, 2005.
Doucleff, Michaeleen. *Hunt, Gather, Parent: What Ancient Cultures Can Teach Us About the Lost Art of Raising Happy, Helpful Little Humans*. New York: Simon & Schuster, 2021.
Eliot, T. S. *Collected Poems 1909–1962*. New York: Harcourt, 1991.
Franks, Christopher. *He Became Poor: The Poverty of Christ and Aquinas's Economic Teachings*. Grand Rapids: Eerdmans, 2009.
Franzen, Jonathan. "Liking is for Cowards. Go for What Hurts." *New York Times*. May 28, 2011. https://www.nytimes.com/2011/05/29/opinion/29franzen.html.
Fukuoka, Masanobu. *The One-Straw Revolution*. New York: New York Review Books, 2009.

Bibliography

Howard, Sir Albert. *The Soil and Health: A Study of Organic Agriculture*. Lexington, KY: University of Kentucky Press, 2006.

Jahrens, Hope. *The Story of More*. New York: Vintage, 2020.

Joerstad, Mari. "The Ground That Opened Its Mouth: The Ground's Response to Human Violence in Genesis 4." *Journal of Biblical Literature* 135 (2016) 705–15.

Klein, Ezra. "Ezra Klein Interviews James Suzman." *New York Times*, June 29, 2021. https://www.nytimes.com/2021/06/29/podcasts/transcript-ezra-klein-interviews-james-suzman.html.

Kundera, Milan. *The Unbearable Lightness of Being*. Translated by Michael Henry Heim. New York: Harper, 1999.

Logsdon, Gene. *Holy Shit: Managing Manure to Save Mankind*. White River Junction, VT: Chelsea Green, 2010.

Logsdon, Gene, and the editors of Organic Gardening and Farming. *A Gardener's Guide to Better Soil*. Emmaus, PA: Rodale, 1975.

Louf, Andre. *The Way of Humility*. Translated by Lawrence Cunningham. Collegeville, MN: Liturgical, 2007.

Laird, Martin, OSA. *Into the Silent Land: A Guide to the Christian Practice of Contemplation*. Oxford: Oxford University Press, 2006.

———. *A Sunlit Absence: Silence, Awareness, and Contemplation*. Oxford: Oxford University Press, 2011.

McKibben, Bill. "130 Degrees." *The New York Review of Books*, August 20, 2020. https://www.nybooks.com/articles/2020/08/20/climate-emergency-130-degrees/.

Montgomery, David R. *Growing a Revolution: Brining the Soil Back to Life*. New York: Norton, 2018.

Montgomery, David R., and Anne Biklé. *The Hidden Half of Nature: The Microbial Roots of Life and Health*. New York: Norton, 2016.

Nickle, Raylene. "Palmer Amaranth Opened the Door to Cover Crops and No-Till on Arkansas Farm." *Successful Famer*, November 26, 2018 https://www.agriculture.com/crops/cover-crops/palmer-amaranth-opened-the-door-to-cover-crops-and-no-till-on-arkansas-farm.

O'Brien, Kevin, SJ. *The Ignatian Adventure: Experiencing the Spiritual Exercises of Saint Ignatius in Daily Life*. Chicago: Loyola, 2011.

Pascal, Blaise. *Pensees*. Translated by A. J. Krailsheimer. New York: Penguin, 1995.

Pfeiffer, Ehrenfied E. *Weeds and What They Tell*. Kimberton, PA: Bio-Dynamic Farming and Gardening Association, 1990.

Rebanks, James. *Pastoral Song: A Farmer's Journey*. New York: Custom House, 2020.

Root, Andrew. *Faith Formation in a Secular Age: Responding to the Church's Obsession with Youthfulness*. Grand Rapids: Baker Academic, 2017.

Sacasas, L. M. "Resisting the Spirit of Babel: Technology, Control and Grace." Unpublished paper presented at the Ekklesia Project, July 9, 2021. Used with permission.

Swenson, Kristen. "Care and Keeping East of Eden: Gen 4:1–16 in Light of Gen 2–3." *Interpretation* 60 (2006) 373–84.

Thurman, Howard. *Jesus and the Disinherited*. Boston: Beacon, 1976.

Tippet, Krista. "Robin Wall Kimmerer: The Intelligence of Plants." February 25, 2016. https://onbeing.org/programs/robin-wall-kimmerer-the-intelligence-of-plants-2022.

BIBLIOGRAPHY

Toensmeier, Eric, and Jonathan Bates. *Paradise Lot: Two Plant Geeks, One-Tenth of an Acre, and the Making of an Edible Garden Oasis in the City.* White River Junction, VT: Chelsea Green, 2013.

Transition Network. *The Essential Guide to Doing Transition: Getting Transition Started in Your Street, Community, Town or Organization.* Totnes, Devon: Transition Network, 2016. https://transitionnetwork.org/wp-content/uploads/2018/08/The-Essential-Guide-to-Doing-Transition-English-V1.2.pdf?pdf=essential-guide-to-transition-v-1.

Von Hildebrand, Dietrich. *Humility: The Wellspring of Virtue.* Nashua, NH: Sophia Institute, 1997.

Walker, Alice. *The Temple of My Familiar.* New York: Amistad, 2010.

Willard, Dallas. *The Great Omission: Reclaiming Jesus' Essential Teachings on Discipleship.* San Francisco: HarperOne, 2006.

Williams, Rowan. *On Christian Theology.* Oxford: Blackwell, 2000.

Wolfe, David W. *Tales from the Underground: A Natural History of Subterranean Life.* Cambridge, MA: Perseus, 2001.

www.ingramcontent.com/pod-product-compliance
Lightning Source LLC
Chambersburg PA
CBHW030113170426
43198CB00009B/612